# Absent from the Body, Present with the Lord

# Absent from the Body, Present with the Lord

Biblical, Theological, and Rational
Arguments against Purgatory

THOMAS J. GENTRY II
*Foreword by David J. Baggett*

WIPF & STOCK · Eugene, Oregon

ABSENT FROM THE BODY, PRESENT WITH THE LORD
Biblical, Theological, and Rational Arguments against Purgatory

Wipf & Stock
An Imprint of Wipf and Stock Publishers
199 W. 8th Ave., Suite 3
Eugene, OR 97401

www.wipfandstock.com

PAPERBACK ISBN: 978-1-5326-5456-5
HARDCOVER ISBN: 978-1-5326-5457-2
EBOOK ISBN: 978-1-5326-5458-9

Manufactured in the U.S.A.                    APRIL 4, 2019

Affectionately and respectfully dedicated to Dave and Jerry

If I ever change my mind on purgatory, it will be your fault.

*Dominus vobiscum*

# Contents

# Foreword

IN EVANGELICAL SUBCULTURE THERE's often a knee-jerk rejection to doctrines of purgatory. Many don't even bother to dignify the discussion with any serious consideration, relegating it to a waste of time. They don't merely reject purgatory or entertain reservations but refuse to subject it to rigorous and careful examination and scrutiny, thinking it unworthy of the time and effort.

When I initially became aware of the thesis of this book—a rejection of purgatory on biblical, theological, and rational grounds—I was skeptical that it would add anything new to the discussion. I was afraid it would offer the same tired talking points, pick some low-hanging fruit, and reinforce the built-in evangelical bias against purgatory.

My friendship with T. J. Gentry should have mitigated those worries and this bias of my own. Although he does at this point come down resistant to purgatory, his is not an attempt merely to tap into prior prejudices or exploit subcultural momentum against the view. His are heartfelt and principled reasons for skepticism, and he endeavors to explicate those reasons in an irenic spirit and rigorous manner. Even still, he is careful to point out at the end of this particular analysis that the discussion is far from over and there's a great deal of fertile material still to discuss, and, as is his wont, he welcomes and encourages such a vigorous exchange.

Readers of all stripes can learn a great deal from this author's warmth and open heart and mind. I know I can. Although, truth be told, I tend to disagree with some of his conclusions—while wholly resonating with others—I accord him and this book accolades for contributing to this important discussion. T. J. is both a dear brother in Christ and a kindred spirit, and I'm confident he won't overly rib me if, on that final day, we find out he was right and I was wrong.

If I'm right, of course, I do intend to rib him endlessly, quite literally. Clearly, he's the better man.

Which reminds me to echo of T. J. Gentry what John Wesley once said of George Whitefield, when asked by a saintly woman, "Dear Mr. Wesley, do you expect to see dear Mr. Whitefield in heaven?"

After a lengthy pause, Wesley replied, "No, madam," to which she wistfully replied, "Ah, I was afraid you would say so."

To which Wesley added, "Do not misunderstand me, madam. George Whitefield was so bright a star in the firmament of God's glory, and will stand so near the throne, that one like me, who am less than the least, will never catch a glimpse of him."

DAVID J. BAGGETT
Lynchburg, Virginia

# Introduction

Why This Book?
An Overview of the Discussion about Purgatory

WHAT HAPPENS WHEN CHRISTIANS die? The official teaching of
the Roman Catholic Church is that, ordinarily, Christians enter
into an intermediate state called purgatory, where they experience
a season of purging from moral impurities that remain in their
souls at the time of death. This purging occurs for varying dura-
tions, based on the type of impurities, to prepare the Christian to
eventually behold the beatific vision of God in heaven.[1] Roman
Catholics are not, however, the only ones who espouse a doctrine
of purgatory. There are also evangelicals who, for reasons different
than traditional Roman Catholics, also conclude that upon death
Christians experience purgatory before actually entering heaven.[2]
These views of purgatory are the subject of discussion that follows.
The argument I hope to make successfully is that the traditional
Roman Catholic and evangelical teachings favoring purgatory are
incorrect for biblical, theological, and rational reasons. I ask the
reader to bear in mind that this work is an introduction to the
topic and a brief one at that. It may prove helpful to think of this
work as a short handbook on purgatory and why it is inconsistent

1. *Catechism of the Catholic Church*, 291–99.

2. Jerry Walls and others are currently advancing this view. Walls's work is
discussed in detail below.

with traditional evangelicalism along biblical, theological, and rational lines of argumentation.

Before we begin, here is a well-intentioned disclaimer: I confess that I am a hat-in-hand evangelical, holding my convictions sincerely but—at least this is my intention—without arrogance or lacking epistemic humility. I am a traditional evangelical, but my heart resonates with the aspects of the "mere Christianity" approach offered by C. S. Lewis, as I consciously recognize that the church is bigger than my convictions, and there are many truths that I hold in common with those I will critique and disagree with in the pages that follow. My purpose is not to unnecessarily offend my Roman Catholic or purgatory-evangelical friends (this is the shorthand phrase I will use throughout to describe them). I am a non-Catholic, but I am not focused on being anti-Catholic. Likewise, I am a non-purgatory-evangelical, but I am not fixated on being an anti-purgatory-evangelical. I am merely entering the conversation that has been going on for many generations. I will make a case against any form of purgatory and in favor of the traditional evangelical position for immediate glorification upon death, and thereby invite further constructive dialogue. I even devote the entirety of chapter 6 to the topic of ongoing discussion. Whether you agree or disagree, let's consider this topic amicably and honestly.

## THE IMPORTANCE OF THE DISCUSSION

This discussion is important for several reasons. Since the time of the Protestant Reformation purgatory has been considered an affront to two critical evangelical doctrines related to authority and salvation.[3] Regarding authority, the Protestant Reformers argued that the Scriptures alone are the final authority for believers in all matters of faith and life (cf. 2 Tim 3:15–17). The doctrine of purgatory, the Reformers argued, is found nowhere in Scripture, but derives instead from corrupted church tradition, and is

3. For a succinct presentation of the fundamental differences between Roman Catholicism and Protestantism, especially as they relate to purgatory, see Allison, "What's the Difference?"

actually contrary to explicit biblical teachings regarding what happens when a believer dies (cf. 2 Cor 5:1–8). Regarding salvation, the Protestant Reformers argued that salvation is by grace through faith alone in Christ (cf. Eph 2:8–9). The Reformers concluded that the Roman Catholic teaching of purgatory, in contradiction to the teaching of faith alone, meant that salvation was a process of works that continued into the intermediate state. Thus, the Reformers concluded that the doctrine of purgatory made salvation a result of human effort.

Additionally, while different from the Roman Catholic approach to purgatory, there are purgatory-evangelicals who are now teaching that it is possible to affirm the doctrines of Scripture's ultimate authority and salvation by faith alone, and still embrace some variation of the doctrine of purgatory.[4] These purgatory-evangelicals, it will be argued, are introducing teachings into the Protestant church that are inconsistent with historical evangelical teaching, and ultimately undermine the authority of Scripture and the sufficiency of the atoning work of Jesus.

Finally, this problem is significant regarding its relationship to the motivations of a growing number of Protestants who are leaving their respective denominations and evangelical beliefs and becoming Roman Catholic.[5] Their reasoning, in some instances, relates to a desire to embrace teachings that are in keeping with the long-standing tradition of the Roman Catholic Church, including purgatory. Sometimes, however, those converting to Roman Catholicism have not been challenged on the unbiblical basis of their new conclusions, nor have they seriously considered the traditional evangelical teaching regarding what happens to Christians when they die. Drawn, as they are, to things in Roman Catholicism such as liturgy, a sense of historical continuity, and the venerable breadth and depth of teaching by those giants of the faith like Augustine, Aquinas, or even contemporary converts like theologian

---

4. Cf. Walls, *Heaven, Hell, and Purgatory*, and *Purgatory*.

5. Cf. Hahn and Hahn, *Rome Sweet Home*. Scott is a former Presbyterian minister who now teaches biblical theology at Franciscan University, Steubenville, Ohio.

Scott Hahn, they leave traditional evangelicalism to board the boat of Rome without considering that there may be barnacles of error attached to the hull.

Personal concerns also motivate me to present this research. As a minister, I often encounter those in the congregation I serve and in other contexts who are unclear on the teachings of Scripture regarding what happens when a Christian dies. Some of these encounters are with those considering the legitimacy of the Roman Catholic doctrine of purgatory, even to the point of contemplating a move into the Roman Church. As a result of these concerns, I have spent considerable time and study involved with this issue, and my conclusion is that there are sound biblical, theological, and rational reasons for rejecting any teaching on purgatory, be it traditional Roman Catholic or purgatory-evangelical.

In my own Christian journey, I was at one time drawn to Roman Catholic teaching and considered leaving Protestantism and becoming Roman Catholic.[6] Thus, I understand, in part, the attraction others feel toward doctrines like purgatory, especially when they are couched in the language of popular apologists like C. S. Lewis or capable philosopher-theologians like Jerry Walls.[7] It is tempting to conclude that if these and other Christians are right on so many other things, perhaps they are right on purgatory. I know the pull of this type of thinking, and I know why I finally resisted it, so my personal story is involved in this discussion, as well. You may agree with me, or maybe you won't, but I believe there are good reasons to reject purgatory and hold fast to the traditional evangelical teaching that at the moment of death a

6. For a one-year period in 2000, this researcher consistently dialogued with former Protestants who converted to Catholicism. This dialogue led him to step away from the pastorate for a season in order to determine if he might actually become Roman Catholic. However, he did not make the move, and returned to his Protestant roots with a renewed zeal and studied conviction regarding the truth of the historic evangelical teachings on the Christian fundamentals, including a rejection of the doctrine of purgatory.

7. Lewis's teaching on purgatory is found, among other places, in his *Mere Christianity* and *The Great Divorce*.

Christian is immediately glorified and ushered into the beautiful presence of God.

## AN OVERVIEW OF THE REASONS
## TO REJECT PURGATORY

Broadly stated, there are biblical, theological, and rational reasons to reject purgatory. All of these are discussed in detail in the chapters that follow and summarized in the appendix. They are introduced here to help frame the discussion (and to give a roadmap to those who like to know where they are headed). Biblically, the Roman Catholic and purgatory-evangelical doctrines of purgatory are in contradiction to the teaching of the Protestant canon of Scripture, and the Roman Catholic teaching, while some attempt to base it in a text from the Apocrypha, does not have explicit apocryphal support. Theologically, both arguments for purgatory are inconsistent with the theological teaching of the sufficiency of Jesus' atonement, undermining the efficacy of both his passive and active obedience in relation to salvation and in contradiction to both Paul's teaching and Jesus' encounter with the thief on the cross. Rationally, both arguments face serious challenges related to human agency, human identity, and the nature of transformation vis-à-vis God's gift of salvation and his purposes in glorification, as well as having logical inconsistencies vis-à-vis the beatific vision and the *Catechism of the Catholic Church*. I will argue, therefore, that only the traditional evangelical understanding of what happens when a believer dies—that he or she immediately enters into the blessedness of God's refreshing presence in perfect holiness—is the proper biblical, theological, and rational position.

## DEFINITIONS, ASSUMPTIONS,
## AND DELIMITATIONS

For the sake of clarity at the outset, the following definitions are offered relative to key terms used throughout this work. The term purgatory is from the Latin *purgare*, meaning to make clean or purify.[8] As used within this work, purgatory refers to the experience of Christians who, upon death, undergo a purging of the remaining effects of sin on their soul. The duration of this purging depends on the severity of the residual forces of sin, and the degree of cooperation between the one being purged and the work of God that accomplishes the purging.

When I use the words traditional evangelicals, I mean those Christians who affirm the sixty-six books of the Protestant canon of the Bible as the final authority in all matters of faith and practice; who profess belief in the triune God who is one in essence and three in eternal persons, Father, Son, and Holy Spirit; who profess that Jesus Christ, the second person of the Trinity, is fully God and fully man, one person with two natures, the human and the divine; who profess that Jesus was born of a virgin, lived a sinless life, died a substitutionary death on the cross, was raised bodily on the third day, and ascended to the right hand of the Father in heaven, from whence he will return bodily and visibly to inaugurate the consummation of God's redemptive work; who profess that at death the Christian immediately enters into an intermediate state where his or her body remains in its final disposition on earth, and his or her soul experiences the presence of God in a paradise-like state, awaiting the final resurrection when body and soul will be reunited and glorified to live in the eternal new heavens and earth; who reject any idea of a purgatorial intermediate state such as taught by Roman Catholics and purgatory-evangelicals.

When I use the description traditional Roman Catholics or Roman Catholics, I am referring to the Roman Catholic teachers who are considered traditionalists in their allegiance to the *Catechism of the Catholic Church* and the Roman Magisterium. Rather than aligning with dissenting Catholics who frequently disagree with official Roman teaching on doctrine or moral issues, these traditionalists are careful to align their biblical exegesis and

---

8. Hanna, "Purgatory." The additional portion of the definition that follows is also from Hanna, with the exception that the evangelical advocates of purgatory focus more on its sanctifying, rather than expiating outcome.

theological teachings with what is considered the official teaching of the Roman Catholic Church.

When I use the words purgatory-evangelical(s), I mean those who accept the majority of the things included in the definition of traditional evangelicals, but profess that it is possible, if not likely, that Christians at death will experience some type of purgatory before the final resurrection and reunion of body and soul. As I explained previously, the term purgatory-evangelicals is not meant to demean or offend; I only use it for the sake of clarity in a discussion that can become confusing at times.

Additionally, the following assumptions apply to the discussion. While there are sound and reasonable defenses for these assumptions, it is beyond the scope of this work to makes such arguments.

I assume the Bible is the infallible, inerrant, authoritative, and sufficient Word of God. As such, it is the ultimate standard by which all doctrine is evaluated, and any tradition that is deemed true is such only insofar as it is consistent with and in submission to biblical teaching (cf. 2 Tim 3:16–17).

I assume that there is an intermediate state that believers enter upon death and consciously experience until the final resurrection; they do not experience soul-sleep while awaiting the final resurrection (cf. 2 Cor 5:5–8).[9]

I assume the traditional evangelical understanding of salvation as given wholly by grace and received by faith alone in Jesus Christ (cf. Eph 2:8–9). Even though the Roman Catholic teaching on salvation differs from the traditional evangelical understanding, the Roman view of salvation will not be directly critiqued, but only insofar as it relates to the Roman understanding of purgatory as an expiatory experience.

I also acknowledge the following delimitations in my presentation. These are the areas I intentionally limit the scope of the discussion for the sake of focus.

The essential consideration of the Roman Catholic view of purgatory will be delimited to the teachings found in the *Catechism*

9. For a consideration of the arguments against soul-sleep, see Calvin, *Soul Sleep*.

*of the Catholic Church* and those sources consistent with its teachings. While there are various teachings found in the contemporary Roman Catholic community regarding purgatory, including those who do not think the doctrine has a place within Catholic thought, only the official teaching of the *Catechism* will be considered.

The primary consideration of the purgatory-evangelical view will focus on the teachings of Jerry Walls, a philosopher and theologian whom I greatly respect and from whom I have learned much—we just don't agree on purgatory.

The commentaries used in evaluating the biblical arguments of those on either side of the issue of purgatory are written from a conservative Roman Catholic or conservative evangelical perspective. Liberal commentators and proponents of higher criticism who do not affirm an elevated view of Scripture's reliability are not considered.

## CONCLUSION

Roman Catholics and some purgatory-evangelicals believe that when a Christian dies his or her soul enters into purgatory so that it might be purified before coming into God's presence in heaven. I intend, through the research presented here, to demonstrate that neither the traditional Roman Catholic arguments nor the purgatory-evangelical arguments represent the best biblical, theological, or rational conclusions. I will argue that the proper understanding of what happens to a Christian at death is the traditional evangelical teaching that the saved soul enters into a pre-resurrection experience of perfect holiness and heavenly rest, awaiting the final reunion of body and soul at the last day. We start in chapter 1 with a summary of the traditional Roman Catholic teaching of purgatory. What saith Rome?

# 1

# What Saith Rome?

## Summarizing the Traditional Roman Catholic Teaching about Purgatory

THIS CHAPTER CONSIDERS THE traditional Roman Catholic teaching about purgatory. I will explain the Roman Catholic teaching in light of its synergistic and sacramental basis, highlight that the teaching rests much of its weight on the distinction between venial and mortal sins and their implication for the temporal and eternal status of the Christian and the all-encompassing Roman teaching regarding initial, ongoing, and final justification.[1]

### THE ROMAN PERSPECTIVE IN CONTEXT

To accurately assess the Roman Catholic teaching about purgatory, it is necessary to consider it within the broader understanding of salvation taught in Roman Catholic theology. The Roman system of redemption may be described as both synergistic and sacramental.[2] It is synergistic insofar as salvation is the outcome of

1. *Catechism*, 543–45.
2. *Catechism*, 304.

divine-human cooperation. While Rome is not teaching that man is the initiator in salvation, or that man can save himself, Rome is teaching that cooperation with the grace of God is implicitly necessary for salvation to be realized. In this regard, Rome and historic Protestantism agree; man must receive the grace of God to be saved. The critical difference, however, is how the cooperation between man and God is realized. Protestantism emphasizes that the essential component in the collaboration is man's faith, while Rome's approach is profoundly different.[3]

This is where the sacramental aspect of the Roman system comes to the fore. Although Rome indeed emphasizes the role of faith in salvation, such belief is indiscernible apart from one's participation in the sacramental life of the Roman Catholic Church. Each sacrament communicates, in and of itself when properly administered, the grace of God, and when a person receives the sacraments by faith, the grace of God within the sacraments and to the person is even more efficacious. For conceptual purposes, the Roman system of salvation may be thought of as planks connecting together to make a walkway, with the sacraments represented by the planks.[4] Each plank is essential to the whole walkway, and each plank helps the person move closer to its ultimate end, to salvation.

At this point, another distinction needs to be explained to better conceive of the Roman understanding of salvation. According to the Roman system, salvation may be thought of as justification experienced in three stages: initial justification, ongoing justification, and final justification. Whereas the Protestant approach generally understands salvation as including justification, sanctification, and glorification, in the Roman system the entire salvific process is about justification, with sanctification and glorification understood as part of the process of justification.[5] This

---

3. *Catechism*, 53–54. One significant difference is the central place of the church in individual salvation.

4. The analogy of planks as the path to salvation in the Roman system is not original to me.

5. *Catechism*, 543.

does not mean that there is no concept of sanctification or glorification in Roman theology, but that for the Roman Catholic the two are part of the broader process of justification, while in Protestant theology sanctification follows justification and concludes in final glorification.

For the Protestant, justification saves the person, sanctification is the process of working out that salvation in holiness of life, and glorification brings the salvation received in justification and demonstrated in sanctification to its two-part culmination—initially at death as the Christian enters the intermediate state awaiting the final resurrection, and conclusively at the final resurrection when Christians receive a glorified body. However, in Roman teaching, the ideas of sanctification and glorification relate to the continual process of justification, with very little if any difference maintained by Rome between justification and sanctification. Rather than the three-part, successive understanding of Protestantism (i.e., justification, sanctification, glorification), in the Roman system initial justification occurs when a person is baptized, and the guilt of original sin is removed, and glorification is the eternal reward of those who achieve final justification through faith and good works.[6]

Building on this clarification, consider the planks of the Roman system of salvation again. Baptism is the first plank, as it washes away the guilt of original sin and provides initial justification. Once baptism is received, ordinarily as an infant in the Roman system, the person is now ready to continue receiving the sacramental grace of salvation. The next plank is reconciliation, also known as confession, where a person makes confession of his or her sin to a priest and then receives absolution.[7] The third plank is communion, by which the person partakes in what Rome teaches is the real body and blood of Jesus as they eat the bread and drink the wine, what has been described as "the source and

---

6. *Catechism.*, 334–42.

7. "It is called the sacrament of forgiveness, since by the priest's sacramental absolution God grants the penitent 'pardon and peace." *Catechism*, 397.

summit of the Christian life."[8] These first three planks, baptism, confession, and communion, provide the ordinary means for a Catholic to experience initial (in baptism) and ongoing (in confession and communion) justification. The fourth plank, which provides yet another means to experience ongoing justification, is confirmation, at which time a person is confirmed publicly in his or her faith as a Catholic and "for the completion of baptismal grace."[9]

There are other sacraments in the Roman system, but they are not universally experienced by all Catholics like baptism, confession, communion, and confirmation. The other sacraments are marriage, ordination, and anointing of the sick (which was ordinarily called 'last rites' by previous generations, since it was usually only done when someone was nearing death).[10] In each of these, when they are properly administered and received, the grace of God for ongoing justification is experienced.

Though there is some internal discussion by Catholics regarding the proper order of the sacraments, some arguing that a child's confession comes before his or her first communion, and some changing that order, all generally agree that the sacraments are of the following types. The sacraments of initiation include baptism, confirmation, and communion. The sacraments of healing include confession and anointing of the sick. The sacraments of service include marriage and ordination.

In addition to the Roman sacramental system, another nuance needs to be explained to lay the groundwork for understanding the Catholic conception of purgatory. In Roman theology, a distinction is made between mortal and venial sins.[11] By mortal sins is meant sins that involve a grave violation of God's moral law with full knowledge of that law and clear intention to violate it. When mortal sins are committed the consequence is that the grace or love that accrues in the soul through faithful participation in

8. *Catechism*, 368.

9. *Catechism*, 358.

10. *Catechism*, 341, 423–24.

11. *Catechism*, 506–9.

the sacramental life is diminished or destroyed. Such destruction is only remediable through a repentant return to the sacraments, especially the sacrament of confession. However, leaving mortal sins unaddressed brings a significant consequence. As the *Catechism* explains, "To die in mortal sin without repenting and accepting God's merciful love means remaining separated from him forever by our own free choice."[12] The outcome described here is none other than hell. To die in a state of unrepentant mortal sin is to be eternally separated from God.

Venial sins are different from mortal sins insofar as, while they involve breaking the moral law of God, they are either minor matters of the moral law, or they involve grave issues that were violated without full knowledge, without a clear intention, or both. Further, whereas mortal sins kill the grace and love of God in the soul, venial sins "do not deprive the sinner of sanctifying grace, friendship with God, charity, and consequently eternal happiness."[13] Thus, mortal sins kill sacramental grace in the soul, while venial sins do not, and unrepentant mortal sins bring eternal separation from God. With this foundation laid, we now consider how the Roman sacramental system and its distinction between mortal and venial sins relates to the doctrine of purgatory.

According to the Catholic scheme, when a Christian commits sin, he or she incurs both an eternal and temporal punishment.[14] The eternal punishment is remitted when the Christian repents and seeks God's sacramental forgiveness. The temporal punishment, be it for mortal or venial sins, still remains. While a Christian may take specific actions in this life to become pure from the effects of sin, to include righteously and patiently enduring the sufferings and trials he or she may face, many will leave this life without being perfectly purified. In such instances, the purification continues after death in purgatory. The *Catechism* states, "All who die in God's grace and friendship, but still imperfectly purified, are indeed assured of their eternal salvation; but after death,

12. *Catechism*, 292.

13. *Catechism*, 508.

14. *Catechism*, 411.

they undergo purification, so as to achieve the holiness necessary to enter the joy of heaven."[15]

If this is so, then how does the Catholic understanding of the relationship between the sacraments, venial and mortal sins, and purgatory, relate to the Catholic understanding of the atonement? Regarding Jesus' atoning death, the *Catechism* explains that "Christ's death is both the *Paschal sacrifice* that accomplishes the definitive redemption of man . . . and the *sacrifice of the New Covenant*, which restores man to communion with God."[16] The *Catechism* goes on to declare that in his work of atonement, "Jesus substitutes his obedience for our disobedience . . . Jesus atoned for our faults and made satisfaction for our sins to the Father."[17]

While it is difficult for me to conceive of any higher or richer description of what Jesus accomplishes on the cross than these words from the *Catechism* regarding Christ's death, there is a significant difference between how Catholics and traditional evangelicals understand the outworking of this accomplishment. This difference between the understandings provides the basis of the response I present in another chapter, but at this point the Catholic position may be simply stated as such: Jesus' perfect obedience in life and his sacrificial death on the cross made full atonement for the sins of man, providing a means for the restoration of communion with God to all who will believe.

According to the Roman system, when a person is baptized the initial benefits of Jesus' life and death are the basis for his or her initial justification, which also enables the person to cooperate with and receive the sanctifying grace of God that is necessary to ongoing justification. Whatever transformation occurs in that person's life is due to the grace of God received synergistically through full participation in the sacramental life of the Catholic Church, and any progress in holiness that person does not make due to the impurities associated with venial and/or mortal sins is, ultimately,

15. *Catechism*, 290.

16. *Catechism*, 175. Italics in original.

17. *Catechism*, 175.

a consequence of that person's choices, since God makes perfect holiness in this life possible.[18]

When a person dies without perfect holiness, assuming he or she does not have unremitted mortal sin, that person will enter into purgatory, where, based on the merit Jesus' atonement provides, they will continue to cooperate with the sanctifying grace of God until they are ready for final justification. On the one hand, purgatory is a consequence for failing to fully cooperate with grace in this life. On the other hand, a person's entrance into and experience of purgatory are based, in the final analysis, on the grace of God made available through the atonement of Jesus Christ. Jesus' death makes salvation possible and purgatory avoidable, but it also guarantees that those who accept the gift of salvation initially will, if they persevere in faith and obedience, eventually receive the final salvation of body and soul in the new heavens and earth.

## CONCLUSION

To summarize, the Roman Catholic teaching regarding salvation and purgatory involves several components, including the sacramental and synergistic process of salvation experienced via the seven sacraments, a distinction between venial and mortal sins and their consequences, and the "now and not yet" aspect of the atonement of Jesus in making salvation possible. For those that do not fully avail themselves of the potential for salvation by achieving holiness before death, purgatory is the final place of purging and preparation for heaven.

Is the traditional Roman Catholic view correct? I don't think it is, and in chapters 3, 4, and 5 I present the biblical, theological, and rational reasons for my rejection of purgatory. However,

---

18. Those who achieve such holiness, or strive fervently and faithfully to that end, are what the Catholic Church refers to as saints. They are not in purgatory, but abide in the fullness of God's presence and serve as intercessors on behalf of the Christians on earth and, possibly, on behalf of the Christians in purgatory. The Catholic Church expresses the distinction between Christians on earth, in purgatory, and in heaven as "The communion of the church of Heaven and Earth." *Catechism*, 270–72.

before I begin my critique, I need to offer a summary of the purga-tory-evangelical position. What saith the purgatory-evangelicals?

# 2

# Evangelicals Believe in Purgatory?

Explaining the Purgatory-Evangelical Teaching

IN THIS CHAPTER, I attempt to summarize Jerry Walls's presentation of the purgatory-evangelical teaching. My principle sources are Walls's books on the topic, though I confess that I cannot do full justice to his thought in this setting. I have, however, attempted to remain faithful to his primary thesis. I realize Walls is not the only Protestant or non-Catholic who affirms some notion of purgatory. Others include C. S. Lewis, H. P. Owen, A. E. Taylor, and David Baggett, all Christian luminaries in the field of philosophy and moral apologetics like Walls. Thus, I confess that I have some trepidation engaging the purgatory-evangelical teaching by Walls and those of the same conviction because it is primarily a philosophical and moral consideration and has been so capably presented by those I mentioned, all thinkers I consider my intellectual betters. To be clear, I do not claim mastery in these areas, which is why I consider my rational critique of purgatory in chapter 5 my tertiary argument, rather than my primary or secondary point of engagement. My current expertise is more biblical and theological, but I do understand how arguments work.

One last caveat before I begin to summarize Walls's teaching. I consider his works critiquing Calvinism as some of the finest ever written, and I personally found them as a lifeline for me out of a hyper-Calvinistic theological box that left me decidedly absent a clear sense of God's love for me or anyone else. God used Dr. Walls to change my thinking and, eventually, to change my life. I am forever grateful to him, which is why it is so difficult to cross sabers, as it were, with him over the topic of purgatory. However, my convictions drive me to write, just as his have inspired him. If he reads my work, I pray that he perceives it as a family discussion around the same evangelical table, and not a personal attack or rejection of his thought *in toto*.

## A SUMMARY OF THE PURGATORY-EVANGELICAL TEACHING

In his book *Purgatory: The Logic of Total Transformation*, Walls, a Protestant, addresses purgatory from multiple perspectives.[1] He considers the historical development of the doctrine of purgatory, including a discussion of objections to the doctrine at the time of the Protestant Reformation. He summarizes the various views of purgatory around three headings: 1) the satisfaction model, which emphasizes the expiatory role of purgatory in making satisfaction for sins (this is the view most closely reflecting the traditional Roman Catholic perspective discussed in the preceding chapter); 2) the satisfaction/sanctification model, which is based on a part expiatory and part transformative understanding of purgatory; and 3) the sanctification model, which, rather than associating purgatory with an expiatory work, focuses on its sanctifying aspects as a means to achieving real existential holiness prior to heaven.[2] Walls also offers his own understanding of purgatory, much influenced by what he describes as the "Mere Purgatory" of C. S. Lewis, and

---

1. For other Protestant pro-purgatory arguments, see Walls, *Purgatory*, chapters 2, 3, and 6.

2. Walls, *Purgatory*, Kindle loc. 1320–2086.

more representative of the sanctification model I just described.[3] Walls views purgatory as the logical extension of God's love in bringing his children to be fully sanctified. He states that "purgatory on this account is not in any way about satisfying divine justice or paying a debt of punishment. It is entirely a matter of continuing and completing the process of sanctification, of making us truly holy so that we can be fully at home in the presence of God and enjoy his presence with no troubling shadows to darken our fellowship with him."[4]

Walls's sanctification approach to purgatory may be summarized as follows. He begins with the admission that purgatory is not explicitly taught in Scripture. However, rather than argue for purgatory from only tradition or philosophy, Walls concludes that "the doctrine is a reasonable inference from things that are clearly taught in scripture."[5] Next, he considers whether or not the doctrine of purgatory is compatible with evangelical theology. Walls argues that the primary concern of the Protestant Reformers was to reject the satisfaction model of purgatory, but that contemporary Roman Catholic theologians, in disagreement with traditional Roman Catholic teaching, tend to view the doctrine more regarding sanctification. (Contemporary Catholics do so even though the *Catechism of the Catholic Church*, as discussed above, clearly identifies purgatory and its attendant works of penance with a satisfactory and expiatory [i.e., justifying] role.)

Walls goes on to point out that there is a debate even within Protestantism about whether or not justification is to be understood in relation to the imputation of Jesus' righteousness, citing disagreements over the various "New Perspectives" on Paul espoused by N. T. Wright and others.[6] For Walls, this provides

3. Walls, *Purgatory*, Kindle loc. 3523–4060.

4. Walls, *Purgatory*, Kindle loc. 1993–2000.

5. Walls, *Purgatory*, Kindle loc. 4090. The word "scripture" is not capitalized in the original.

6. Walls, *Purgatory*, Kindle loc. 4101–16. In this regard, Walls cites Wright, *Justification*. Additional works related to the question of the imputation of Jesus' righteousness include Smith, *Eternal Covenant*, and Wilkins and Garner, eds., *Federal Vision*.

the impetus to argue for an approach to justification that makes sanctification and justification closely related, such that the entire salvific enterprise appears to me to be more akin to a process of becoming saved than a declaration of salvation in justification that results in its outworking through sanctification and its culmination in glorification.[7] In his final analysis regarding the possible compatibility of purgatory and evangelical theology, Walls concludes that there is enough variance within evangelical teaching to allow for purgatory. In what I conclude is a bit of an oversimplification by Walls, he states that "Protestants who still object to the doctrine of purgatory tend to conceive of salvation primarily in terms of justification, whereas those who are more sympathetic to the doctrine tend to stress sanctification and the transformational dimensions of God's work to save us."[8]

This brings Walls to his conviction that the entire discussion of purgatory is inextricably linked to how human freedom interplays with God's work of grace in sanctification. Walls declares that "the most crucial matter on which the whole issue turns [is], namely, what role does our free response play in our salvation . . . Is it necessary for us truly and actually to become holy that we undergo a process of moral transformation in which we freely cooperate, or can this transformation be effected by a unilateral, instantaneous act of God the moment we die?"[9] For Walls the answer is clear: if God chooses, as in the traditional evangelical formulation of what happens upon a Christians' death, to immediately complete the work of sanctification and perfect the believer in holiness (what is sometimes described as the "zap" approach), then God is doing something inconsistent with human freedom and true love. If God were to carry out this type of instantaneous work producing holiness, Walls is concerned that humans would not recognize themselves, and that such immediate change is not in keeping with the necessity of temporal, successive and progressive, incremental transformation. Rather, Walls emphasizes that purgatory,

7. Walls, *Purgatory*, Kindle loc. 4116.

8. Walls, *Purgatory*, Kindle loc. 1249.

9. Walls, *Purgatory*, Kindle loc. 4119.

not God's direct action, produces the genuine transformation that preserves free moral agency.[10]

Walls concludes his explanation of purgatory by asking whether or not God is willing to do everything short of coercion to bring men and women to salvation, including the possibility that purgatory provides an opportunity for postmortem conversion and probation. According to Walls, this would allow those Christians who do not achieve perfect sanctification in this life, something Walls appears to consider possible, an opportunity to continue to grow in grace in a postmortem state. Further, nonbelievers who might have come to saving faith with more time and influence can possibly be saved if there is a purgatory or some sort of further opportunity in the intermediate state. Two of Walls's statements reveal his thoughts on these matters more clearly. Regarding the opportunity purgatory affords to believers, he states:

> If there is a perfectly good God, there is reason to hope that our lives will not end in death or ultimate futility, but rather that our lives have ultimate meaning. There is reason, moreover, to hope that our moral efforts are not in vain, that good will triumph . . . not only on the cosmic scale, but in our own individual lives . . . This reminds us one more time that purgatory, properly understood, is not an alternative to grace, but is itself an expression of grace.[11]

Regarding the possibility of postmortem conversion for unbelievers, Walls offers this explanation: "I have been arguing that the doctrine of purgatory makes best sense of how . . . Christians who die far short of perfection, as well as others who have not yet accepted Christ, can be appropriately transformed and fitted for heaven."[12]

So, there it is, an honest attempt to summarize Wall's position on purgatory. To reiterate, he offers several points of explanation in making his purgatory-evangelical case.

10. Walls, *Purgatory*, Kindle loc. 4126.
11. Walls, *Purgatory*, Kindle loc. 4140–54.
12. Walls, *Purgatory*, Kindle loc. 4070.

1. Though not explicitly found in Scripture, purgatory is a reasonable inference from what is taught in the Bible about God's love, human freedom, and holiness.

2. When understood from the perspective of sanctification rather than justification, purgatory is also consistent with the tenets of historic Protestant orthodoxy.

3. Since there is a lack of consensus on the understanding of Christ's imputed righteousness, and since not all Protestants speak of salvation exclusively in terms of justification, purgatory is a reasonable option for Protestants.

4. Purgatory is a necessary concomitant with a believer's lack of complete sanctification in this life, his essential human identity, and the love of God, since an instantaneous transformation upon death would transgress human freedom and moral agency.

5. Given God's loving nature and his desire to see all saved and in right relationship with him for eternity, purgatory affords believers a probation of sorts in which to fully participate in God's loving transformation even after death; and may imply some type of postmortem conversion opportunity for those God knows would choose him if they just had the right chance and circumstances, even after death.

## CONCLUSION

It is not only Roman Catholics who espouse some teaching of purgatory. As we have seen, evangelicals like Jerry Walls offer articulate, challenging arguments in favor of purgatory, though for differing reasons from traditional Roman Catholicism. What, then, is a traditional evangelical to say to these things?

Are the views of traditional Roman Catholics correct regarding purgatory? Are the views of Walls and other notable Protestants correct in their purgatory-evangelical views? I don't think they are, and in the next three chapters I will present my reasons.

Chapter 3 focuses on the interpretation of several key biblical texts and one apocryphal text related to purgatory. Chapter 4 presents theological reasons to reject purgatory, and chapter 5 presents rational reasons to reject it. So, let's begin with the biblical and apocryphal texts. What saith the Lord?

# 3

# Are They Correct in Their Interpretation of the Text?

Textual Reasons to Reject Purgatory

THIS CHAPTER BEGINS WITH a consideration of biblical and apocryphal texts that provide reasons to reject purgatory.[1] The biblical texts are Malachi 3:2–4; Matthew 5:25–26; Matthew 12:31–32; Luke 16:19–31; 1 Corinthians 3:10–17; and John 14:1–4. The apocryphal text is 2 Maccabees 12:38–46. With the exception of John 14:1-4, each text is interpreted according to a pro-purgatory perspective, which concludes that these texts either directly or by implication support the doctrine of purgatory. Next, a traditional evangelical response argues that, rather than supporting purgatory, each of these texts is better interpreted as doing one or more of the following: speaking of the eternal state of heaven or hell; employing literary devices such as euphemism; or looking to the

---

1. It is beyond the purview of this thesis to consider the legitimacy of the Apocrypha and why it is not included in the Protestant canon of Scripture. However, as will be argued, the apocryphal text in question can be engaged on its own merits from a hermeneutical perspective. While the apocryphal text provides a relatively small portion of the overall discussion, it is included due to its centrality to the traditional Roman Catholic position.

final resurrection and final judgment. The foci of the traditional evangelical responses are to show that, unless approached with an *a priori* commitment to the doctrine of purgatory, there are reasonable non-purgatory interpretations possible and likely for each text.

## MALACHI 3:2–4

> 2 But who can endure the day of His coming? And who can stand when He appears? For He *is* like a refiner's fire and like launderers' soap. 3 He will sit as a refiner and a purifier of silver; He will purify the sons of Levi, and purge them as gold and silver, that they may offer to the LORD an offering in righteousness. 4 Then the offering of Judah and Jerusalem will be pleasant to the LORD, as in the days of old, as in former years.[2]

We begin our consideration with Malachi 3:2–4, where the prophet describes "the day of His coming," when God will "purify the sons of Levi, and purge them as gold and silver, that they may offer to the LORD an offering in righteousness." The broader context speaks of a messenger who prepares the way for God's coming to purify and purge his people (v. 1), and that the outcome of the cleansing will be that God accepts his people's offerings and brings judgment against further impurities (vv. 4–6).

Advocates for purgatory interpret Malachi 3:2–4 as providing the basis for purgatory by way of implication, even though they acknowledge that the passage likely refers to the final judgment. Francis de Sales, for example, notes that early church fathers such as Origen, Ambrose, Augustine, and Jerome understood this passage as a reference to the end of time, but that the need for a final purging as described in the passage is an acknowledgment that purging is required, in general, before coming into the presence of God in heaven.[3] Thus, what Malachi speaks of is a specific refer-

---

2. Unless otherwise noted, all Scripture quotations are from the New King James Version.

3. de Sales, *Catholic Controversy*, 358.

ence to one purging at the end of time for those who are alive at the final resurrection, but Malachi also provides, by way of implication, the basis for purging of those who die before the final day. God's concern, according to this interpretation, is to demonstrate his commitment to purging his children, not to describe a one-time event on the final day.

However, arguing for purgatory by way of implication from the Malachi passage requires an *a priori* commitment to reading more into the text than is there. As Keil and Delitzsch explain, rather than implying a doctrine of purgatory, the Malachi passage speaks of purification and purging in the sense of "judgment upon the godless members of the covenant nation," such that God's people are purified and purged by the removal of the wicked from their midst.[4] While this is still purging, the emphasis in the passage is on God's purifying work at a particular moment in the life of the covenant nation, not on anything postmortem. Further, rather than describing preparation of someone to enter the presence of God, the passage primarily speaks of punishing those who will never come into his presencce. There is also a purifying of the people of God implied in this passage, but it is the priests of Levi who are Malachi's focus for purification since national revival for Israel would require a restoration of true worship as led by a righteous priesthood. Such renewal is viewed by Malachi as future, pointing most likely to the future Messianic kingdom.[5]

It is true that any interpretation of this passage that focuses on the text must affirm that God is purging his people to make them righteous. However, what God is purging is wicked people from their midst, not necessarily wickedness from within them; while God certainly makes his people holy, personal sanctification is not the focus of this passage. Again, only by reading an *a priori* commitment to purgatory into the text is it likely to find in this passage support for purgatory. Recognizing that there is a purging

4. Keil and Delitzsch, *Commentary on the Minor Prophets*, Kindle loc. 15932.

5. Keil and Delitzsch, *Commentary on the Minor Prophets*, Kindle loc. 15955.

process described is not the same as demonstrating that the passage teaches purgatory. The most that could be concluded without an *a priori* commitment is that the passage describes a purification process and that purgatory is also a purification process; that is as far as the relationship between Malachi and any teaching about purgatory legitimately goes.

## MATTHEW 5:25–26

> 25 Agree with your adversary quickly, while you are on the way with him, lest your adversary deliver you to the judge, the judge hand you over to the officer, and you be thrown into prison. 26 Assuredly, I say to you, you will by no means get out of there till you have paid the last penny.

The next biblical text related to the discussion of purgatory is Matthew 5:25–26. In this text, Jesus urges his disciples to resolve conflicts quickly, lest they end up in "prison" (v. 25), a place they will not leave until they "have paid the last penny" (v. 26). The broader context of the passage is Jesus' teaching that murder begins with anger in the heart (v. 22), and that conflict with a brother or sister provides an impediment to worship that requires reconciliation before worship may be restored (vv. 23–24).

Proponents of purgatory interpret Matthew 5:25–26 as a warning from Jesus that those who refuse to reconcile with their adversaries will undergo some type of punishment that will last until the appropriate payment is made. The penalty, according to this interpretation, is purgatory. Tertullian, for example, interprets this passage as a warning of purgatory for minor offenses, based on Jesus' use of the word translated "penny" in verse 26.[6] Just as the penny is a small amount of money, so the punishment and purification of purgatory are for lesser sins. Tim Staples notes that the Greek word translated "prison" in verse 25 is the same word used in 1 Peter 3:19 to describe the holding place of the "spirits in prison, who formerly were disobedient" in the days of Noah, a

6. Tertullian, *Treatise on the Soul*.

place which Staples concludes is purgatory.[7] Thus, to go to prison is to go to purgatory, and only after paying the full amount (i.e., being purified) will the person find release and, by implication, enter into heaven.

The problem with the pro-purgatory interpretation of the Matthew passage is not that it finds a message of judgment in the words of Jesus, but that it concludes that such judgment is purgatory, instead of eternal separation from God at the final judgment. Rather than interpreting this text as an allegory for purgatory, a non-purgatory interpretation is based upon an understanding that Jesus' words involve an allegory about eternal separation from God. When speaking of being "thrown into prison" (v. 25), and "by no means get[ting] out of there till you have paid the last penny" (v. 26), Jesus communicates the idea that if the judgment he warns of is actually experienced, it will be experienced forever. Michael Wilkins explains that "remaining imprisoned until a debt is repaid down to the last penny elicits a sense of impossibility (v. 26; cf. Matt. 18:34) since the debtor had no chance to work to create funds."[8]

Craig Blombergconcludes that Jesus is warning of the judgment of hell, not purgatory, arguing that the force of the passage within its broader context is directed to the importance of living reconciled with others and avoiding God's final wrath on judgment day for an unrepentant, murderous heart.[9] Wilkins adds that the gist of Jesus' words is that his disciples must always seek reconciliation, rather than allow unreconciled anger to destroy a relationship, whether with brothers (vv. 23–24) or "adversaries" (vv. 25–26).[10] Refusing to pursue this type of radical reconciliation is tantamount to murder, against which great judgment will be meted out on the final day, revealing that those with murderous hearts were not actually true followers of Jesus (cf. Matt 7:21–23). Does the passage in Matthew 5 speak of judgment? Certainly.

7. Staples, "Is Purgatory in the Bible?"

8. Wilkins, *Matthew*, 243.

9. Blomberg, *Matthew*, 108.

10. Wilkins, *Matthew*, 243.

However, the judgment it points to is better understood as hell, not a place of purging to better prepare someone for heaven.

## MATTHEW 12:31–32

> 31 Therefore I say to you, every sin and blasphemy will be forgiven men, but the blasphemy *against* the Spirit will not be forgiven men. 32 Anyone who speaks a word against the Son of Man, it will be forgiven him; but whoever speaks against the Holy Spirit, it will not be forgiven him, either in this age or in the *age* to come.

The *Catechism of the Catholic Church* references Matthew 12:31–32 in support of purgatory, so it is the third biblical text for consideration.[11] In this passage, Jesus speaks to his disciples regarding what is often described as "the Unpardonable Sin." Jesus is making the point that blasphemy against the Spirit (i.e., a denial of the overt work of God through Christ by attributing it to the power of Satan) "will not be forgiven men . . . either in this age or in the age to come" (v. 32).[12]

Advocates of purgatory interpret the ages Jesus speaks of in Matthew 12:32 (i.e., "this age . . . the age to come") as references to this life and the intermediate state between death and the final resurrection. As the *Catechism* explains, "As for certain lesser faults, we must believe that, before the Final Judgment, there is a purifying fire. He who is truth says that whoever utters blasphemy against the Holy Spirit will be pardoned neither in this age nor in the age to come. From this sentence we understand that certain offenses can be forgiven in this age, but certain others in the age to come."[13] Consistent with this interpretation, Roman Catholic interpreter George Haydock explains that the passage teaches "that some sins may be remitted in the world to come; and consequently

---

11. *Catechism*, 291. In making this reference, the *Catechism* draws upon the *Dialogues* of Gregory the Great, bk. 4, ch. 39.

12. See Grudem, *Systematic Theology*, 1237.

13. *Catechism*, 291.

that there is a purgatory, or a middle place."[14] So, according to the pro-purgatory interpretation of this passage, certain sins against Jesus may be forgiven in this age or in purgatory, but when one blasphemes the Holy Spirit, he or she will not receive forgiveness in either one.

However, interpreting Matthew 12:31–32 in a manner supportive of purgatory fails to recognize both the Jewishness of the immediate context and the help the broader synoptical context brings to the interpretive task.[15] Don Stewart explains that the phrase "in this age or in the age to come" is a Jewish euphemism for "never," not something intended to cryptically introduce the idea that there is the possibility of forgiveness for specific sins and not others in a future purgatorial intermediate state.

Further, as Stewart also discusses, in the Synoptic Gospels (cf. Mark 3:29; Luke 12:10) the language Jesus uses regarding blasphemy is very precise, omitting any reference to two ages, probably since Mark and Luke are writing to Gentiles not necessarily familiar with Jewish euphemisms. In Mark 3:29 Jesus states that "he who blasphemes against the Holy Spirit never has forgiveness, but is subject to eternal condemnation," and in Luke 12:10 he declares that "to him who blasphemes against the Holy Spirit, it will not be forgiven." Rather than finding purgatory in Matthew 12:31–32, careful consideration of the immediate and broader canonical context reveals that Jesus is making clear that blasphemy is a severe and damnable offense. As with previous passages of Scripture, the pro-purgatory interpreter must begin with an *a priori* commitment to the doctrine to find support for purgatory in Matthew 12:31-32.

## LUKE 16:19–31

> 19 There was a certain rich man who was clothed in
> purple and fine linen and fared sumptuously every

14. Haydock, *Commentary on the New Testament*, Kindle loc. 2521.

15. The argument in this paragraph is a summary of Stewart, "Is There Any Biblical Support for Purgatory?"

day. 20 But there was a certain beggar named Lazarus, full of sores, who was laid at his gate, 21 desiring to be fed with the crumbs which fell from the rich man's table. Moreover the dogs came and licked his sores. 22 So it was that the beggar died, and was carried by the angels to Abraham's bosom. The rich man also died and was buried. 23 And being in torments in Hades, he lifted up his eyes and saw Abraham afar off, and Lazarus in his bosom. 24 Then he cried and said, "Father Abraham, have mercy on me, and send Lazarus that he may dip the tip of his finger in water and cool my tongue; for I am tormented in this flame." 25 But Abraham said, "Son, remember that in your lifetime you received your good things, and likewise Lazarus evil things; but now he is comforted and you are tormented. 26 And besides all this, between us and you there is a great gulf fixed, so that those who want to pass from here to you cannot, nor can those from there pass to us." 27 Then he said, "I beg you therefore, father, that you would send him to my father's house, 28 for I have five brothers, that he may testify to them, lest they also come to this place of torment." 29 Abraham said to him, "They have Moses and the prophets; let them hear them." 30 And he said, "No, father Abraham; but if one goes to them from the dead, they will repent." 31 But he said to him, "If they do not hear Moses and the prophets, neither will they be persuaded though one rise from the dead."

Luke 16:19–31 is another biblical text for consideration. Therein, Jesus tells the story of a beggar named Lazarus and an unnamed rich man. The beggar was beset with sores (v. 20), and begged crumbs from the rich man's table (v. 21), while the rich man enjoyed fine apparel and meals (19). Both men died, and the rich man is described as being in torment (v. 23), while Lazarus is "carried by the angels to Abraham's bosom" (v. 22), where he is comforted (v. 25). The rich man begs for mercy from Abraham but is told that nothing will be done to relieve his suffering (v. 26), nor will anything be done to warn his family members to avoid judgment, since they already had the word of God in "Moses and the prophets" (vv. 29, 31).

Interpreters who affirm purgatory appeal to this passage in support of their views based on the following.[16] First, Abraham calls the rich man who is in torment "son," and the rich man calls Abraham "father," imploring him for mercy. This language only makes sense, according to the pro-purgatory interpretation, if there is actually a family relationship between the rich man and Abraham, which implies that the rich man is being punished but has not been forever cut off from the blessings of Abraham. Thus, the rich man is in purgatory. Second, the rich man demonstrates genuine concern for his loved ones (vv. 27–28) and a recognition that what is needed to avoid such suffering is repentance (v. 30). How, the pro-purgatory interpreter asks, are such qualities possible in the soul of someone who is in hell? Rather than viewing the rich man as in hell, he should be considered to be in a transitional state

---

16. Hahn, "Purgatory." Here are a few of Hahn's specific thoughts on the rich man and Lazarus in Luke . "It may not be amiss likewise to find signs of this moral amelioration in the rich man in Hades who appeals to Abraham on behalf of his five brothers still on earth, in Luke 16. Remember the story of Lazarus and the rich man? The rich man is in fire, but he calls out, 'Father Abraham,' and Abraham responds, 'My son, or my child.' Well all that man had done was to feast sumptuously. He didn't go around beating Lazarus and other poor people. He just ate sumptuously. He neglected the poor. Not a mortal sin in and of itself, to be sure. And he says, 'Father Abraham . . . Have mercy on me. He didn't say, 'This is unfair. I shouldn't be in hell.' He says, 'Have mercy on me. Just get Lazarus to dip his little finger tip in water and put it on the tip of my tongue. I don't deserve it, but it's mercy.' Is that a soul in hell filled with the hatred of God? St. Teresa says, 'There is no love in hell.' And yet, this man pleads, not on his own behalf, but he says, 'Please send Lazarus back to my five brothers so that they will believe in time.' Abraham says, 'Even if a man came back from the dead, it wouldn't be enough. They've got Moses, the law and the prophets. That's enough.' But ironically, who did Jesus raise from the dead? A man named Lazarus. And was it enough for the Jews to believe in Jesus then? No. They not only wanted to kill Jesus, they even sought to kill Lazarus because so many people were still believing in Jesus because of him. But look at Luke 16 and realize that this man is there for neglecting the poor. He is in fire, recognizing Abraham as his father. Abraham recognizing him as [his] child. This man pleading for mercy in the form of a drop of water and then pleading on behalf of his brothers who were still on earth. Do souls intercede with God for mercy? Hardly. And yet look at what the story assumes. Look at what Jesus doesn't even feel it necessary to argue."

in purgatory, where the reform of his will is already taking place in the descriptions Jesus gives.

The problems with the pro-purgatory interpretation in the Luke passage are varied.[17] Pro-purgatory advocates assume that what Jesus describes is an actual occurrence between two real people with details that should be interpreted literally and in favor of purgatory. Rather than considering that this passage could be a parable and that the description of the interaction between Lazarus and the rich man is intended to communicate a parabolic lesson about rich and poor, unbelief and belief, the purgatory interpretation hinges on the unproven assumption that the story is literal, and the details are speaking of purgatory, even though the passage is couched in a section of Luke containing several other parables (cf. Luke 15:1—16:13; 18:1–14). While the intention of Jesus as literal or parabolic is unclear, there is indeed no clear basis to conclude this a literal account, nor that it is teaching purgatory. At best, the purgatory interpreters are right that the passage teaches something about judgment and reward.

Advocates of purgatory also fail to explain the nature of the rich man's sins, although the broader context emphasizes a lack of faith and repentance on the part of the rich man and his family (vv. 29–31). Even the rich man's attitude toward Lazarus reveals he still sees Lazarus as subservient to him (v. 24, "send Lazarus to me that he may dip the tip of his finger in water and cool my tongue"), and that he thinks he knows better than Abraham and refuses to submit to his judgment (v. 30, "No, father Abraham; but if one goes to them from the dead, they will repent."). These are more than the minor sins that purgatory is supposed to address, which means that if the rich man is in purgatory then the pro-purgatory interpretation introduces the possibility that someone can either be in a saving relationship with God in spite of entrenched unbelief and unrepentance or that it is possible to experience postmortem conversion. These options ultimately undermine the doctrine of hell by either redefining the necessity of faith and repentance in

17. The response related to the Lukan passage reflects the input of Michael Chiavone, professor at Liberty University..

salvation (contrary to passages such as John 3:16 and Acts 2:38–40) or by extending into the postmortem state the opportunity to receive salvation (contrary to Heb 9:27). Though I know of no Roman Catholic accounts for postmortem conversion that are within the pale of Catholic orthodoxy, purgatory-evangelicals such as Walls do appear to leave open this possibility. Their argument is not explicitly based on a biblical text but derives more from their understanding of God's love and the philosophical implications they deem it bears on matters of eternal destinies. More on this is discussed in chapter 5.

Further, the descriptions of the postmortem experience of Lazarus and the rich man present a stark contrast between the rest Lazarus enjoys (v. 25) and the intense, apparently irremediable suffering the rich man endures (v. 26). Regarding the rich man, there is no clear redemptive emphasis in the passage; instead, the focus is on reward and punishment in the postmortem state. The rich man wants relief and receives none; he wants to tell his family of his suffering but is not allowed. It appears he gets no quarter from his judge. Robert Stein concludes that the broader Lukan context (cf. Luke 6:20, 24) reveals Jesus' message of the "blessedness of the poor believer [as a recipient of the kingdom of God] . . . and the woe of the unbelieving rich [who receive their consolation in this life]."[18] This distinction between blessedness and rest for the believing poor, of which Lazarus is undoubtedly an example, and the temporal consolation from wealth but postmortem punishment for unbelief and unrepentance in the unbelieving rich, of which the rich man is an example, do not require a pro-purgatory interpretation. The emphasis in Luke 16:19–31 is, instead, the need for repentance and faith, and the promise of God's presence with those who suffer righteously. As in the case of examples discussed above, only an *a priori* commitment to purgatory would provide the basis for interpreting the account of the rich man and Lazarus in a pro-purgatory manner.

18. Stein, *Luke*, 422.

# 1 CORINTHIANS 3:10–15

> 10 According to the grace of God which was given to me, as a wise master builder I have laid the foundation, and another builds on it. But let each one take heed how he builds on it. 11 For no other foundation can anyone lay than that which is laid, which is Jesus Christ. 12 Now if anyone builds on this foundation *with* gold, silver, precious stones, wood, hay, straw, 13 each one's work will become clear; for the Day will declare it, because it will be revealed by fire; and the fire will test each one's work, of what sort it is. 14 If anyone's work which he has built on *it* endures, he will receive a reward. 15 If anyone's work is burned, he will suffer loss; but he himself will be saved, yet so as through fire.

First Corinthians 3:10–15 presents Paul's admonition that the work of Christian ministry must be conducted with great care, coupled with a warning that God will judge those who bring harm to his church. Paul communicates this message using the image of a builder who must carefully construct his building on the foundation that is already laid by another (vv. 10–11), and who must do so with the most valuable and enduring materials (vv. 12–13). Paul warns that a fiery judgment will one day reveal the quality of each person's work in building (v. 13), resulting in reward for faithful builders (v. 14), and loss of reward for unfaithful builders (v. 15a), though the builder "himself will be saved, yet so as through fire" (v. 15b).

Arguing that in this passage, especially verse 15, "the [Roman Catholic] Church has found a foundation for its doctrine of purgatory," George Montague explains that Paul's emphasis here is on the purging and purification that each person will experience in purgatory.[19] The fiery trial Paul speaks of is not limited to the final judgment (i.e., "the Day" in v. 13), but describes the regular experience of believers, especially those who do not exercise their gifts and callings with faithfulness. In his argument for a purgatorial meaning for the judgment of v. 15, Roman Catholic commentator

---

19. Montague, *First Corinthians*, Kindle loc. 1500.

Haydock concludes that "the Day" may be understood as "either the day of general judgment, or the particular judgment, when everyone is judged at his death, which sentence shall be confirmed again at the last day," and this dual meaning, therefore, provides the basis for which "divers of the ancient fathers, as well as later interpreters . . . prove the Catholic doctrine of a purgatory."[20]

While I do not deny that Paul is discussing some type of positive or negative judgment related to individual works, what Paul describes is, as demonstrated by the emphasis Paul places on the judgment occurring on "the Day," a once-and-final event in every believer's future (or at least every minister's future, since the passage is focused on how one proceeds to work in helping build the church of God). As one who does not think Paul intends to provide a basis for purgatory, Dan Mitchell agrees. He interprets 1 Corinthians 3:10–15, especially verse 15, as a warning of the judgment some Christians will receive on the last day if their work of ministry is found lacking in substance.[21] Mitchell explains that Paul is not talking about a loss of salvation for those who receive the judgment, nor is he talking about an extended season of purging, but a sudden loss of reward related to ministry.[22]

Michael Chiavone adds, "The man himself is never said to be in the fire. It is the man's work which is manifested by fire, remains, or is lost."[23] Mark Taylor also concludes that Paul's concern is the final loss of reward that some Christian workers will experience, since Paul's use of "the Day" in verse 13 "refers to the eschatological day of judgment" in the sense of the judgment at the end of time.[24] In support of this conclusion, Wright explains that Paul's broader concern is that the Corinthians understand that there is continuity between this age and the next, a continuity that is demonstrated in how well one's work endures at the resurrection and judgment that come at the end of this age; Paul's emphasis is on the future

20. Haydock, *Commentary on the New Testament*, Kindle loc. 15995–16008.

21. Mitchell, *Book of First Corinthians*, 55.

22. Mitchell, *Book of First Corinthians*, 55.

23. Adapted from my personal correspondence with Dr. Chiavone.

24. Taylor, *1 Corinthians*, Kindle loc. 2289–2300.

moment of resurrection and transition that will usher in the final judgment and the new heavens and new earth.[25]

In their interpretation of this passage, Mitchell, Chiavone, Taylor, and Wright represent a consensus that acknowledges a final judgment resulting in reward and loss related to works, but nothing intended to substantiate a doctrine of purgatory. Once again, a pro-purgatory interpretation of this passage requires an *a priori* commitment to the idea of the need for sustained purging before entering God's presence. Both pro- and anti-purgatory advocates acknowledge in this passage some type of judgment associated with the final consummation, but a sustained period of purging must be read into the passage if one finds it there.

## JOHN 14:1–4

> 1 Let not your heart be troubled; you believe in God, believe also in Me. 2 In My Father's house are many mansions; if *it were* not *so*, I would have told you. I go to prepare a place for you. 3 And if I go and prepare a place for you, I will come again and receive you to Myself; that where I am, *there* you may be also. 4 And where I go you know, and the way you know.

The final biblical text for consideration is John 14:1–4, wherein Jesus seeks to comfort his disciples in light of his coming departure. He senses that they are uneasy about the future, even fearful, and his words of comfort speak of what he will do for them when he departs. As he explains in verse 2, "In My Father's house are many mansions; if it were not so, I would have told you. I go to prepare a place for you."

Although I did not find a single pro-purgatory interpretation of this passage, it is included in the discussion for the possible explanation it offers regarding the nature of the intermediate state the believer experiences between death and the final resurrection. Consider the insights of Wright, who explains that the word Jesus uses for "mansions" is from the Greek *mone*, "a temporary

---

25. Wright, *Resurrection of the Son of God*, 284–85.

resting-place, or way-station, where a traveler would be refreshed during a journey."[26] As Wright further details, the idea in Jesus' words draws from Jewish apocalyptic writing related to the "chambers in which souls are kept against the day of eventual resurrection," providing a safe resting place between death and the final resurrection at the last judgment.[27] Thus, when a believer dies, she enters into an intermediate state of rest and refreshment, enjoying her *mone* as she awaits the final resurrection. These observations by Wright, rather than supporting the idea that the intermediate state is a place of purging, provide insight into God's gracious intention in providing a place of rest and refreshment for those awaiting the final judgment. Such rest and refreshment are hardly consonant with the idea of a purging fire of redemptive suffering for those who "sleep" in Christ (cf. 1 Thess 4:14). To suffer while one sleeps is to endure a nightmare, and nightmares are hardly consonant with what Jesus promises his followers in John 14:1–4.

One may object at this point that the passage in question is not about the intermediate state, but about the final resurrection and the new heavens and new earth. If this is true, then Jesus' words would have no direct bearing on the purgatory discussion since neither pro-purgatory position argues that after the final consummation there will be suffering in heaven; the suffering they speak of is before and a prerequisite for heaven. However, while I recognize that my application of Wright's insights concerning the believer's *mone* are possibly novel, it is defensible that what Jesus offers in this passage is hope and consolation for his disciples while they await his return for them at some future time—possibly his second coming, but more likely at the time of their death and entrance into the intermediate state. I think it strains logic to think that the disciples would hear Jesus speak of a *mone*, something they would surely have been familiar with as Jews in the period of Second Temple Judaism amid the burgeoning apocalyptic and messianic expectations in their immediate culture, and draw this conclusion: Jesus is telling us that we should have hope while he

26. Wright, *Resurrection of the Son of God*, 446.
27. Wright, *Resurrection of the Son of God*, 446.

is gone because he will return for us in the end, and then take us to a temporary resting place while we await the final resurrection. Rather than conflating the *mone* with the final resurrection, I think it makes sense if they anticipate that they will die and be with Jesus before the final resurrection, at which time they will enjoy their *mone*. Again, to think that they hear Jesus speak of something temporary and associate it with the final resurrected state strains logic and seems to me incredulous. This is why Wright's insight vis-à-vis intertestamental Jewish apocalyptic literature is so helpful. Heaven in the intermediate state is a place of rest—a *mone*—where believers will repose and await the final resurrection. Purging and rest are not the same things, any more than going to a weight loss camp to become fit and lose weight is the same as a long, relaxing stay at a top resort. Words matter and Jesus' use of *mone* is telling.[28]

Before considering the passage in 2 Maccabees 12, I offer these conclusions regarding the brief review of biblical texts thus far. It seems to me that pro-purgatory interpreters consistently bring an *a priori* commitment to purgatory to their interpretation of the text, leaving them open to the charge that they are guilty of a variation of proof-texting-by-way-of-implication to support a previously held conclusion. Likewise, the entire notion of purgatory as a place of purging and redemptive suffering militates against the direct words of Jesus regarding his intention to make a place of refreshment and respite for his followers as they await the final resurrection. But Roman Catholics have additional books in their Bible, books known as the Apocrypha. What do those books say about purgatory? The apocryphal text of 2 Maccabees 12:38–46 will now be evaluated relative to this question.

28. Ed Christian's research into the Jewish expectation of Sheol in the Jewish mindset of Jesus' day reveals that the expectation of faithful Jews was a time of rest with their fathers already awaiting the resurrection, while the wicked would be separated from their fathers. Thus, within Sheol there were believed to be two sections separated by an uncrossable divide, one side for the righteous and one for the wicked. This connection is certainly consistent with Wright's discussion of the mone. See Christian, "Rich Man and Lazarus."

## 2 MACCABEES 12:38–46

The primary ancient source relied upon by the *Catechism of the Catholic Church* is the text in 2 Maccabees. As the *Catechism* states, "This teaching [of purgatory] is also based on the practice of prayer for the dead, already mentioned in Sacred Scripture: 'Therefore [Judas Maccabeus] made atonement for the dead, that they might be delivered from their sin.' From the beginning, the Church has honored the memory of the dead and offered prayers in suffrage for them . . . so that, thus purified, they may attain the beatific vision of God."[29] The reference made by the *Catechism* is to 2 Maccabees 12:38–46, quoted here in its entirety:

> 38 Judas rallied his army and went to the city of Adullam. As the seventh day was approaching, they purified themselves according to custom and kept the sabbath there. 39 On the following day, since the task had now become urgent, Judas and his companions went to gather up the bodies of the fallen and bury them with their kindred in their ancestral tombs. 40 But under the tunic of each of the dead they found amulets sacred to the idols of Jamnia, which the law forbids the Jews to wear. So it was clear to all that this was why these men had fallen. 41 They all therefore praised the ways of the Lord, the just judge who brings to light the things that are hidden. 42 Turning to supplication, they prayed that the sinful deed might be fully blotted out. The noble Judas exhorted the people to keep themselves free from sin, for they had seen with their own eyes what had happened because of the sin of those who had fallen. 43 He then took up a collection among all his soldiers, amounting to two thousand silver drachmas, which he sent to Jerusalem to provide for an expiatory sacrifice. In doing this he acted in a very excellent and noble way, inasmuch as he had the resurrection in mind; 44 for if he were not expecting the fallen to rise again, it would have been superfluous and foolish to pray for the dead. 45 But if he did this with a view to the splendid reward that awaits those who had

29. *Catechism*, 291.

gone to rest in godliness, it was a holy and pious thought.
46 Thus he made atonement for the dead that they might
be absolved from their sin.

The passage speaks of the actions of Judas Maccabeus upon finding that a number of his comrades fell in battle, presumably because they wore amulets associated with idolatry. Upon discovery of the amulets Judas did two things specifically relevant to the existence of purgatory, according to the traditional Roman Catholic interpretation. First, he prayed that the sins of the warriors be removed. Second, he collected an offering and sent it to Jerusalem so that sacrifice could be made on behalf of the fallen. These two actions he performed with a view to the final resurrection, wanting to make sure that the sins of the fallen were absolved postmortem so that they might enjoy the reward of the just on the day of resurrection.

Based on these actions by Judas, the *Catechism*, as stated above, establishes its "scriptural" basis for purgatory. Without addressing why the text of 2 Maccabees is not considered Scripture from the Protestant perspective, the question of the meaning of the text can be asked. How, precisely, does what Judas did provide a sufficient basis for establishing the doctrine of purgatory? To conclude that purgatory is supported herein requires the following assumptions. First, it is necessary that the reader assume that as a result of their sins the fallen were in a state of purging until the final resurrection. Second, it must be supposed that the purpose of the expiatory offering made in Jerusalem was to relieve postmortem suffering. Without these two assumptions, is it reasonable to conclude the doctrine of purgatory? I don't think it is reasonable.

Here is the problem with these two assumptions. The first assumption has no support in the text since a postmortem experience of purging and redemptive suffering is not mentioned here or anywhere in the Maccabean corpus. It is just not there. The second assumption misses the clear statement in the text regarding the reason for Judas's sacrifice.[30] As verse 43 explains, the purpose of

---

30. Adapted from the insights of Michael Chiavone.

the sacrifice was Judas's concern for the final resurrection, demonstrated by these words: "in doing this [sacrifice] he acted in a very excellent and noble way, inasmuch as he had the resurrection in mind." Again, nothing in the text speaks of a state of postmortem purging, but the resurrection is clearly in view, and this is in keeping with both the Maccabean and prophetic understanding of a future resurrection followed by a final judgment.[31] Consider, for example, the words of Daniel 12:2 that there is coming a day when "many of those who sleep in the dust of the earth shall awake, some to everlasting life, some to shame and everlasting contempt." Daniel's emphasis is similar to the focus in 2 Maccabees, the final resurrection.

Thus, the two assumptions necessary for the purgatory interpretation of 2 Maccabees do not hold up under closer scrutiny. There is nothing explicit in the text about postmortem purging, and the focus of Judas was directed to the future resurrection. Whether he had theological grounds for this action is also not the topic of discussion, but what does matter is that Judas never mentions (nor does anywhere else in Maccabees) a connection between the prayer he made or the sacrifices he paid for and purging during the intermediate state. Further, the text speaks of the future resurrection as belonging to "those who had gone to rest in godliness" (v. 45), implying that if there was any concern in Judas's mind regarding heaven, it was that the fallen were, to use an evangelical idea, saved and on the way to heaven. Judas may believe in postmortem salvation via sacrifice by others on behalf of the fallen, but this is different from purgatorial suffering in preparation for the final resurrection.

To tie the argument for the doctrine of purgatory so closely to 2 Maccabees 12:38–46 requires what I think are unwarranted assumptions on the part of the interpreter and, ultimately, I do not think the passage can bear the weight of the doctrine it allegedly supports. What may be stated for sure about the passage in 2 Maccabees 12:38–46 is that sin was committed, and people died,

---

31. For a more thorough discussion of the role of resurrection in Maccabean thought, see Wright, *Resurrection of the Son of God*, 150–53.

and a pious leader offered prayers and sacrifice on behalf of the dead in light of his belief in the final resurrection and his desire that the fallen would enjoy its blessings. Again, nothing in the passage speaks of a purgatorial state. This is why Roman Catholics like J. Cevetello tellingly admit that "In the final analysis, the Catholic doctrine on purgatory is based on tradition, not Sacred Scripture."[32]

## CONCLUSION

In this chapter, I considered the biblical and apocryphal texts related to the doctrine of purgatory. Although many advocates of purgatory attempt to find support for their position in the Bible and/or Apocrypha, I presented arguments that I think demonstrate that none of the biblical or apocryphal texts overtly or necessarily support any teaching of purgatory. Further, I argued that it is only through failure by the advocates of purgatory to avoid unwarranted *a priori* commitments that a conclusion in support of purgatory is even possible. I also sought to demonstrate that what Jesus intends for his followers when they enter the intermediate state between death and the final resurrection is a place of rest and respite, not a place of purging and redemptive suffering. Moving from these textual reasons for rejecting purgatory, in the next chapter I present several theological reasons against purgatory that bear on both traditional Roman Catholics and the purgatory-evangelicals. Are the advocates of purgatory correct in their theology?

32. Cevetello, "Purgatory: In the Bible," 825.

# 4

# Are They Correct
# in Their Theology?

Theological Reasons to Reject Purgatory

IN THIS CHAPTER, I offer theological reasons to reject both the
traditional Roman Catholic and purgatory-evangelical teachings
regarding Christians in the intermediate state. In brief, the reasons
are: purgatory contradicts Paul's teaching regarding what happens
to a Christian at death; it diminishes the significance of the passive
obedience of Jesus Christ and its implications for justification; it
diminishes the significance of the active obedience of Jesus Christ
and its implications for sanctification; and it fails to account for the
promise of Jesus to the thief on the cross.

## PURGATORY CONTRADICTS PAUL'S
## TEACHING REGARDING WHAT HAPPENS
## TO A CHRISTIAN AT DEATH

I believe the doctrine of purgatory should be rejected because
it contradicts the Pauline teaching regarding what happens to
a Christian at death. Paul declares in 2 Corinthians 5:7–8 the

following: "For we walk by faith, not by sight. We are confident, yes, well pleased rather to be absent from the body and to be present with the Lord." Paul urges the Corinthians to be confident that when the physical body dies the believer will be with the Lord. Commenting on this passage, David Garland explains, "The picture [Paul] paints shows that as soon as we are away from the physical body we are present with the Lord in a new dimension that is qualitatively different from our experience of the Lord's presence in the body."[1] To affirm that purgatory is the "qualitatively different . . . experience of the Lord's presence" that Paul has in mind, the pro-purgatory perspective must completely ignore the broader context of Paul's words, and it is difficult to see how purgatory is far more comforting and glorious. Quite the opposite.

For clarity, consider Paul's teaching in light of his words in 2 Corinthians 4:7–18. Paul reminds the Corinthians that his ministry is beset with struggling and difficulty, even to the point of "always [being] delivered to death for Jesus' sake" (v. 11). Paul knows that this "light affliction, which is but for a moment, is working for us a far more exceeding and eternal weight of glory" (v. 17). What is the glory of which Paul speaks?[2] He explains in 2 Corinthians 5:1–8, using several contrasts to speak of the greatness of the glory to come versus the temporary difficulty he faces in this life: his earthly home will be replaced with a heavenly one (v. 1); he will be clothed in such a way that he will not be naked, but "further clothed" (vv. 2–4a); his mortality will be "swallowed up by life"

---

1. Garland, *2 Corinthians*, Kindle loc. 5052.

2. Gardland and Hodge discuss at length the possibility that the greater glory Paul writes of could be that, at death, Christians actually receive some form of a glorified physical body, rather than entering into God's presence in a disembodied state. Garland argues that this is what Paul means, and that the intermediate body will be further glorified at the final resurrection, while Hodge argues that the language used by Paul is not focused on a body that is glorious, but an experience that is glorious; the Christian experience at death, argues Hodge, is entrance into a glorified state in which the soul is immediately glorified, and which will conclude at the resurrection when the body is finally glorified. Either way, glory is the focus, not purging. See Garland, *2 Corinthians*, Kindle loc. 4815–89; and Hodge, *Commentary on 2 Corinthians*, Kindle loc. 1822–63.

(v. 4); he is "at home in the body" and "absent from the Lord" in the sense that what the Spirit is given as a guarantee of (i.e., future glory; cf. Rom 8:23) will begin when Paul is with the Lord on the other side of death (vv. 5–6).

This is why, flowing from these varied contrasts, Paul declares his commitment to "walk by faith, not by sight" (v. 7), since what is to come is far greater than what is; when he leaves this body in death he will be with the Lord in a qualitatively different experience of life (v. 8). As John Wesley explains in commenting on verse 8, "This demonstrates that the happiness of the saints is not deferred till the resurrection."[3] The final resurrection will be glorious indeed (cf. 1 Thess 4:15–18), but those who die in the Lord before that time will also enjoy a glorious experience in God's presence (2 Cor 4:17).

Charles Hodge's words are also helpful here. "Into [the Lord's] presence the believer passes as soon as he is absent from the body, and into his likeness the soul is at death immediately transformed."[4] This confidence of what is to come compels Paul to focus on his manner of life and conduct, so that he is "well pleasing" (v. 9) to the Lord as he looks toward death and the final judgment (v. 10). In making this transition from the hope of a Christian's being with the Lord upon death to a focus on the final judgment of all people, Paul is placing the experience of believers at death within the broader context of cosmic eschatological concerns. Paul is saying that Christians must always live in light of the final day, a time in which God will judge all people, Christians and non-Christians.[5] In the meantime, as Christians see their own deaths approaching,

---

3. Wesley, *2 Corinthians*, Kindle loc. 508.

4. Hodge, *Commentary on 2 Corinthians*, Kindle loc. 1943.

5. I agree with Hodge that verse 11, rather than being directly related to verse 10 in the context of the final judgment, actually begins a new but related thought in Paul's argument. Paul's emphasis in verse 11 on persuasion is, according to Hodge's approach, is in keeping with Paul's desire to defend his integrity to those in Corinth who were doubting his apostolic authority. Paul's point is that, in light of the final judgment of all people, and his desire to be with Christ when he dies, he would not compromise his integrity; there was too much at stake. See Hodge, *Commentary on 2 Corinthians*, Kindle loc. 2023–40.

they may take comfort that "to be absent from the body [is] to be present with the Lord" (v. 8).

Before considering more carefully the traditional Roman Catholic approach to these verses, it will help to summarize Paul's teaching relevant to 2 Corinthians 5:7–8. Paul is making the case that when Christians suffer in this life, God uses the suffering to prepare them for greater glory (2 Cor 4:7–15). Further, when Christians die they will leave their body and be in the presence of the Lord, experiencing that greater glory (vv. 1–8). Therefore, Christians must commit to live faithfully until they go to be with the Lord, always keeping in mind that there is a final judgment coming for all people (vv. 9–11). In all this, Paul does not teach anything about a purgatorial experience after death.

It is not, however, that Catholics do not offer an interpretation of Paul's words. Catholic commentator Haydock interprets Paul's words with a clear commitment to the doctrine of purgatory. Haydock writes regarding verse 8:

> *We are absent from the Lord*, and as it were pilgrims. He compares the condition of men in this mortal life with that of pilgrims far from their own beloved country, yet with hopes to arrive there, which makes them willing to undergo dangers, and makes Christians even resigned to death, to a separation of the body from the soul, that they may *be present with the Lord*, and enjoy him. But let everyone reflect that he must be judged, and receive a reward or punishment *according* to his works.[6]

Notice that Haydock does not comment on the substance of Paul's words about being present with the Lord as soon as he is absent from the body. Instead, he interprets Paul's message as a demonstration that Christians are willing to undergo anything, even "separation of the body from the soul," to be with the Lord.

This is undoubtedly true, but, as discussed above, Paul is saying more than something about the willingness of Christians to suffer for a greater ultimate purpose and destination; he is

---

6. Haydock, *Commentary on the New Testament*, Kindle loc. 17487. Italics in original.

making a statement of what happens when a believer leaves this life through death. A believer dies and is with the Lord. Granted, the traditional Roman Catholic is not denying that Jesus is with his children as they endure purgatory, so a pro-purgatory advocate could argue, though this author is not aware of any that do, that "with the Lord" means with Jesus in the midst of purgatory, but such a conclusion still conflicts with Paul's teaching that what comes after death is glorious. Only the traditional Roman Catholic's *a priori* commitment to the doctrine makes it possible to find it in this text, and even then it contradicts the broader context, which emphasizes that suffering in this life is used by God to prepare Christians for the greater glory they will experience as soon as they leave this body in death and enter into God's presence.

In a different but related pro-purgatory interpretation, Thomas Stegman, writing in the *Catholic Commentary on Sacred Scripture*, explains Paul's words as expressing his desire to be with the Lord when he leaves the body, but not necessarily making a declaration of what will happen.[7] Rather than interacting with the direct words of Paul in verse 8, Stegman concludes his commentary on verses 1–9 by explaining that "because it is not up to [Paul] when he will pass on from this life, he sets forth in [v.] 9 his fundamental attitude in the here and now: **we aspire to please him**."[8] However, while it is the case that Paul gives emphasis to the importance of pleasing the Lord, his concern to do so is not motivated by Paul's uncertainty of his destination upon death, but precisely because Paul is so confident that he will be with Jesus in glory when he dies.

Consonant with the general Catholic emphasis on works and judgment in relation to purgatory discussed above, Stegman interprets Paul's words not in keeping with the passage's hopeful and confident emphasis, but in a way that leaves open the possibility that Paul himself was headed to purgatory, even though he wanted to go to be with the Lord; nonetheless, Paul, according to Stegman, was committed to the best attitude. Both Haydock and Stegman

7. Stegman, *Second Corinthians*, Kindle loc. 2530.

8. Stegman, *Second Corinthians*, Kindle loc. 2530. Bold in original.

appear to be consistent with traditional Roman Catholic teaching, but by avoiding actually commenting on Paul's specific words in relation to his broader context, and, instead, reading conclusions into the text, I conclude that they miss the meaning of Paul's teaching. The words in 2 Corinthians 5:7–8 are contrary to, not supportive of, the doctrine of purgatory.

## PURGATORY DIMINISHES THE SIGNIFICANCE OF JESUS' PASSIVE OBEDIENCE

In addition to what I find as its incongruity with Paul's teaching just discussed, I further conclude that the teaching of purgatory, especially the traditional Roman Catholic doctrine, diminishes the significance of the passive obedience of Jesus Christ and its implications for justification. The passive obedience of Jesus refers to his willingly accepting the wrath of God on the cross and bearing the guilt of the sins of the world. Grudem explains, "In addition to obeying the law perfectly for his whole life on our behalf, Christ also took on himself the sufferings necessary to pay the penalty for our sins."[9] The emphasis with passive obedience is primarily, though not exclusively, on the death of Jesus, and active obedience, which is discussed next, is mainly about the life of Jesus.[10] How, then, does Jesus' passive obedience relate to purgatory in the traditional Roman Catholic scheme?

By maintaining that purgatory exists for the sake of completing the purification process a person does not complete in this life, and that the purification process relates to the sin of the person, be it venial or mortal, I think Rome necessarily implies that Jesus' passive obedience was insufficient since the key to purgatorial purification is primarily through human works of penance and

---

9. Grudem, *Systematic Theology*, 571.

10. As Grudem discusses, some object to the distinction between passive and active obedience, noting that all Jesus' obedience was active. However, the distinction does help distinguish between what Jesus did in living obeying the law (active obedience) and what Jesus did in receiving the penalty for disobeying the law (passive obedience). See Grudem, *Systematic Theology*, 527, fn. 3.

their alleged satisfactory and expiatory value, rather than the imputation of the merits of Jesus' passive obedience to the believer. Instead of finding completion in the work of Jesus on the cross, Rome's teaching leads to the conclusion that Jesus only makes the first step of purification, and that the person must then follow on with his or her own actions to move from initial, to ongoing, to final justification.

The *Catechism*, in discussing the death of Jesus on the cross, states that "in the redeeming love that always united [Jesus] to the Father, he assumed us in the state of our waywardness of sin, to the point that he could say in our name from the cross: 'My God, my God, why have you forsaken me?'"[11] However, if Jesus truly identified with fallen humanity in experiencing being forsaken by God due to sin, and if the wrath of God was truly poured out upon Jesus in that state of identification, why is there still a need for purgatory, or for any acts of penance in this life or in purgatory that attempt to remit sins that were supposedly dealt with on the cross?[12] The Catholic answer is that conversion is not just a once-for-all event; initial conversion occurs in baptism, and ongoing conversion occurs in a continual commitment to the sacrament of confession and the concomitant requirement of penance, since Christians are "at once holy and always in need of purification, [and are to follow] constantly the path of penance and renewal."[13]

As discussed above, it is through the sacrament of confession and its necessary penance that the sinner is able, insofar as he does true works of penance that involve contrition, confession, and satisfaction, to "recover his full spiritual health" and "make satisfaction for or expiate his sins."[14] Notice that it is the penitent who makes satisfaction and expiation through his or her works.

11. *Catechism*, 171.

12. *Catechism*, 406–7. It is important at this point to recognize that repentance, which is clearly described as the appropriate response of the Christian to sin (cf. 1 John 1:8–9) is not the same as penance. According to the *Catechism*, penance is the proof of repentance, whereby a person makes reparation for his or her sins through prescribed acts that merit forgiveness and restoration.

13. *Catechism*, 398.

14. *Catechism*, 407.

While Catholics may respond that what the penitent does is in union with Jesus, it is still the person who accomplishes this by their own actions, rather than enjoying the blessings of satisfaction and expiation freely given in Jesus by virtue of his perfect passive obedience.

In the Roman system, Christians are always needing purification and continuously on the path of penance if they are to ever behold the glories of heaven. This is not, however, in keeping with the biblical account of the imputation of Christ's righteousness to all who believe, since, as Paul makes clear in Romans 4:25, the Son of God "was delivered up because of our offenses, and was raised because of our justification." If this is true, where is the need for penance or purgatory? The passive obedience of Jesus makes these things unnecessary and, in light of what Scripture explains that the death of Christ accomplished it is understandable how some conclude that purgatory is offensive to the gospel.

## PURGATORY DIMINISHES THE SIGNIFICANCE OF JESUS' ACTIVE OBEDIENCE

As mentioned earlier, active obedience refers to the life Jesus lived in perfect submission to and fulfillment of God's law. Grudem explains that "Christ had to live a life of perfect obedience to God in order to earn righteousness for us. He had to obey the law for his whole life on our behalf so that the positive merits of his perfect obedience would be counted for us."[15] Think of it this way: what passive obedience secures concerning justification, active obedience demonstrates and applies in the life of the believer concerning sanctification.

However, in much the same way way purgatory undermines the significance of passive obedience, I also conclude that it diminishes Jesus' active obedience. Purgatory makes both the death and life of Jesus insufficient means for the believer to be made entirely right in his or her standing with God. For the sake of discussion,

15. Grudem, *Systematic Theology*, 570.

allow that somehow the passive obedience of Christ only made initial justification possible, removing the guilt and penalty for all sins committed to the point of initial conversion. Does it not follow that the active obedience of Christ, his perfect righteousness, would benefit the believer in securing his or her ongoing and final justification, making the Christian life more about gracious growth in Christlikeness than about purging, satisfying, and expiating?

Here, again, is what I find as the fundamental flaw in the Roman Catholic soteriological system (and I conclude that the purgatory-evangelical position regarding sanctification comes near this same problem): Jesus enables much for the believer, but he actually accomplishes nothing for sure, since a person's faith and good works are the final basis upon which salvation/glorification is received. This appears to me to be contrary to Paul's teaching in Ephesians 2:8–10, wherein he clearly explains that salvation is by God's grace, received through faith and not accomplished by works, even though works certainly follow as a product of, but not the cause of, salvation.

Likewise, rather than merely making something possible for the believers, somehow enabling them to merit salvation but not actually accomplishing it for them, the writer of Hebrews uses definite salvific language in Hebrews 9:12, explaining that it was "not with the blood of goats and calves, but with His own blood [that Jesus] entered the Most Holy Place once for all, having obtained eternal redemption." Jesus has obtained redemption, not merely made it possible. As with the negative impact I find it makes on Jesus' passive obedience, so purgatory presents what I think is an offense to the gospel message that is revealed in Jesus' active obedience.

Two comments from Martin Luther offer his insight into why why he found purgatory an unacceptable teaching. Notice how both of the comments are relevant to the discussion of the passive and active obedience of Jesus. In his lectures on Genesis, delivered in 1535, Luther states that "purgatory is the greatest falsehood because it is based on ungodliness and unbelief; for they deny that faith saves . . . We die in faith in Christ, who died for our sins and rendered satisfaction for us."[16] Luther also addresses purgatory in one of his Table Talks, declaring, "as for purgatory, no place in Scripture makes mention thereof, neither must we in any way allow it; for it darkens and undervalues the grace, benefits, and merits of our blessed, sweet Savior Christ Jesus."[17] These statements demonstrate that for Luther it is in Jesus that the completion of salvation is found, and in Jesus alone.

## PURGATORY FAILS TO ACCOUNT FOR THE PROMISE OF JESUS TO THE THIEF ON THE CROSS

Though sometimes overlooked or understated, the significance of the account of Jesus and one of the thieves crucified with him in Luke 23:32-43 also provides what I find to be a strong argument against purgatory. The setting of the passage is Luke's crucifixion narrative, and Luke describes one of the thieves as hostile and disrespectful to Jesus, while the other defends Jesus (vv. 39–40). The thief who defends Jesus goes on to confess that he and the other thief are guilty and deserve their punishment, but Jesus "has done nothing wrong" (v. 41). After making his confession of guilt and professing Jesus' righteousness, the thief asks Jesus to remember him upon coming into his kingdom; Jesus replies with a promise that "today, you will be with Me in Paradise" (v. 42). The term "Paradise" has Old Testament precedent referring to a grove of trees or a garden (cf. Gen 13:10; Eccl 2:5), and in the New Testament sometimes speaks of the final resting place of the righteous (cf. 2 Cor 12:24; Rev 2:7), although Wright explains that it could also indicate a temporary resting place.[18] Either way, in Luke's passion narrative Paradise is where Jesus is going, and he promises to take the thief along, the implication being that Paradise is a place

16. Luther, *Lectures on Genesis Chapters 21–25*, 424.

17. Luther, "Of Purgatory."

18. See Wright, *Resurrection of the Son of God*, 438; and Stein, *Luke*, 593.

of rest. I find nothing even remotely purgatorial about what Jesus promises to the thief.

This is relevant to Walls's purgatory teaching in the following two ways. First, there is no indication in the text, nor do I find sufficient warrant, to draw the conclusion that the thief was wholly sanctified before his death. This man was a condemned criminal, and by his own admission he was guilty of the crimes and deserving of the punishment he was receiving. His conversion on the cross certainly brought him to Jesus, but the man did not have time to undergo what Walls describes as the necessary, incremental, actual growth in experiential holiness before death. Yet, Jesus promises the man will be at rest in Paradise that very day, presumably as soon as he dies. How can this be unless Jesus was also going to entirely sanctify this man in holiness as he passed from death into Paradise?

This reveals the second way in which the experience of the thief is relevant to Walls's teaching: it portrays the man's free choice of Jesus and, I think necessarily implies that Jesus was going to transform the man and make him fit for Paradise as part of the salvation the man willingly received. The man chose Jesus and, as a gracious consequence, Jesus decided to change the man. As will be discussed below, I fear that Walls creates an unnecessary bifurcation between freedom and the act of God in instantaneously completing a Christian's sanctification at death by concluding that freedom and such direct acts are irreconcilable. I, however, think that, the thief on the cross is an example of just this sort of human freedom interwoven with God's choice to glorify his children when they die.

## CONCLUSION

What are the theological problems I find with the traditional Roman Catholic and purgatory-evangelical teachings about purgatory? I conclude that both Rome and the purgatory-evangelicals contradict Pauline teaching about a believer's experience at the moment of his or her death, both undermine the sufficiency of

Jesus' passive and active obedience, and that the purgatory-evangelical position fails to account for Jesus' promise to the thief on the cross. (I recognize that it is possible that a Roman Catholic could claim that the thief's obvious repentance and faith demonstrate a sort of baptism-by-tears that would leave him without need of purging since he died immediately thereafter without committing post-baptismal sins. If, for the sake of argument this is granted as at least consistent with the Roman system, then the thief on the cross is more of a problem for purgatory-evangelicals than Catholics.) Having considered my biblical and theological reasons for rejecting the teaching of purgatory, in the next chapter I present rational reasons to reject it. Are the advocates of purgatory correct in their reasoning?

# 5

# Are They Correct in Their Reasoning?

Rational Reasons to Reject Purgatory

IN THIS CHAPTER, I move away from the biblical and theological considerations regarding purgatory, focusing instead on the logic of my pro-purgatory interlocutors. At times I will touch on biblical and theological matters, but the primary concern is exposing what I think are some of the rational inconsistencies in the traditional Roman Catholic and purgatory-evangelical positions. For example, aspects of the pro-purgatory position involve philosophical anthropology, which is the study of human nature and touches on matters such as free will and moral transformation and other ethical considerations. While I do not address philosophical anthropology, per se, I do discuss a logical concern of the purgatory-evangelical argument that centers on philosophical anthropology. To be clear, my presentation in this chapter is far from exhaustive, and, as I stated in the opening of chapter 2, this is my tertiary argument. Like a doctor who "practices" medicine, my arguments in this chapter are exploratory and tentative, though I do think they have merit and provide additional strength to my overall rejection of purgatory. What, then, are the rational reasons to reject purgatory?

## PURGATORY UNNECESSARILY OPPOSES FREE WILL AND INSTANT GLORIFICATION

I find that the purgatory-evangelical position creates unnecessary opposition between human freedom and the work of God in instantaneous glorification at the moment of a believer's death. According to Walls, libertarian freedom is given a place that is second only to the non-coercive love of God. Walls does not accept that it is in keeping with God's loving disposition to immediately and unilaterally complete one's sanctification at the process of death since doing so appears to deny the role of human freedom in what he concludes is necessarily incremental and gradual growth in holiness. Walls appears to hold that it is impossible to have true freedom and instantaneous transformation in the same person's experience. If God does it instantly, you and I are not fully involved, and the change is somehow inconsistent with true human transformation.

There is a certain gravitas to Wall's position at this point, and I do agree that some attempts to explain glorification minimize the human aspect and tend to reduce final sanctification to something that happens to me, rather than in me. However, I do not think that one must abandon the traditional evangelical teaching of instantaneous glorification to preserve human-divine synergy. Thus, I reject the concern about human freedom and glorification for the following reasons.

The idea that sanctification must be gradual and incremental, while it may be true in the experience of many Christians, is in no way universally true or necessary. Any consideration of Christian testimonies reveals that for some people, coming to faith in Christ brings an immediate and abiding change in who they are, how they think, and what they do. Obviously, this is the expectation, since according to Paul in 2 Corinthians 5:17, "if anyone is in Christ, he is a new creation; old things have passed away; behold, all things have become new." Purgatory-evangelicals may object at this point by noting that Paul's description concerns justification, not sanctification. I will grant this, but this objection only removes the problem one level. So, I ask, why is it not acceptable to make definitive, immediate moral transformation at the end of a Christian's life, but it is acceptable to do so at conversion? In both instances moral transformation is in question, so why not object to the transformation at conversion, too, since moral transformation necessarily involves a human's will? I conclude that there is a choice made, even in the instantaneous transformation that occurs in many conversions. The person chooses to let God change them, and he does.

Is it not assumed when one comes to Christ that he is trusting God to finish what he started, and is there not an implicitness to the process of sanctification like that of justification—that I cannot ultimately do for myself what only God can do? Of course there is, and just as it is not inconsistent with my human free agency to willingly submit to a doctor to perform a surgery on me while I am passive and under anesthesia, so it is not against my free will to choose to let God do what he chooses in an instant; this is what I agree to and graciously receive in my conversion. I am asking that God change me because I cannot change myself. I submit to the lordship of Jesus and his total control of my being, even looking to him for my transformation (see Gal 2:20). Does this vitiate my identity and make me unrecognizable? No. I still recognize who I am in my humanity after my conversion, even though something was done to me instantaneously and unilaterally upon my choice, and I will still recognize who I am in my humanity if God instantaneously glorifies me upon my death.

Another problem I find with the pro-purgatory position that freedom of will is incompatible with an instantaneous, divine transformation of a person at death has to do with a further nuance of what it means to submit to Christ's lordship. As a question the problem may be considered as follows: What if the initial request for Christ to forgive, save, and transform includes with it the person's implicit acceptance (even if not consciously so) that

God will complete sanctification at the moment of death? There is nothing contradictory in this idea, and it has been the fundamental testimony of evangelical Christians for centuries.

As a necessary corollary to this historical testimony, I hasten to add that just because I accept what has been the default position among evangelicals since the time of the Reformation it does not attain that I am simply adopting the default for the sake of preserving status quo. There is a reason evangelical teaching has held together in its fundamental core for so long, and if one considers the way the Holy Spirit often accomplishes his doctrinal work in the church through consensus over centuries, there is also a good indication that the Holy Spirit is at work in the shared testimony of evangelicals regarding this issue. Does historical consensus prove a doctrine's correctness? No, but historical consensus does matter, and removing the ancient boundaries is no small concern. Lest one conclude that it is in the spirit of Protestantism to do just that, and so the more power to the purgatory-evangelicals, I ask one question: Do the purgatory-evangelicals really think their concern carries the same gravitas as the fundamental matters of the Reformation concerning the authority of God's Word and the manner of salvation by faith alone? I don't think they do, but to resist an evangelical consensus because it has come to be the default position in this matter appears possibly reckless and without sufficient warrant.

Consider Paul's words in Philippians 2:12–13, "work out your own salvation with fear and trembling; for it is God who works in you both to will and to do for His good pleasure." Notice the emphasis on working out salvation (i.e., the process of sanctification) knowing that God is the one at work for his good pleasure. Is there a human-divine synergy? Yes, and there will be until we take our last breath, and then the Lord finishes what he started by completing the transformation. Let us not forget that Paul also proclaimed in Philippians 1:6 that God, "who has begun a good work in [us] will complete it until the day of Christ Jesus." Every believer is God's work to complete. This is why the traditional evangelical position powerfully resonates across the centuries regarding God's work of instantaneous glorification at the moment of a believer's death. As the *Westminster Confession of Faith* explains regarding the disposition of a Christian's soul upon death, "The bodies of men, after death, return to dust, and see corruption; but their souls (which neither die nor sleep), having an immortal subsistence, immediately return to God who gave them. The souls of the righteous, being then made perfect in holiness, are received into the highest heavens, where they behold the face of God in light and glory, waiting for the full redemption of their bodies."[1] The unilateral work of God in accomplishing this is a product of the initial choice to receive his lordship; there is no contradiction.

## PURGATORY OBFUSCATES THE SIGNIFICANCE OF THE BEATIFIC VISION

One of the joys of heaven is to see God face to face, to behold what has been termed the beatific vision—the blessed vision of God in glory. First John 3:2 speaks of the power of this encounter, exclaiming that "we know that when He is revealed, we shall be like Him, for we shall see Him as He is." These words of John follow his reminder that we Christians are already children of God, but that there is a mysterious transformation in our future. When we see Jesus, we will become like him (analogically, not univocally!). Why? Beholding his visage is the means to radical transformation. That's right, seeing Jesus in heaven transforms the believer in a manner that is beyond description. While the traditional Roman Catholic and purgatory-evangelical both emphasize the need to prepare and be transformed in a postmortem manner before Christians may see God, it seems to me that the Bible tells us that the transformation comes upon seeing God. The beatific vision changes me, rather than me needing to go through purgatorial suffering so that I can be changed to see the beatific vision. Just think through this for a moment. Purgatory reverses the process,

---

1. *Westminster Confession of Faith*, XXIII.I.

forgetting that what transforms us is God's glorious presence, not a process of postmortem suffering.

Some may object at this point, claiming that purgatory only prepares us to behold the beatific vision. Yes, the advocate of purgatory claims, the vision may further change us, but we have to get ready to be changed before we can be changed. In response to this, I ask: Is this not a bit like cleaning up to take a bath? I think so, and, further, I do not think the pro-purgatory objection attains because it only removes the concern one level. Here's how: if I grant that my transformation into a glorified child of God is finally completed when I encounter the beatific vision, then I am granting that there will be an instantaneous change in my person. The question is no longer whether I will be instantaneously changed, but when. Thus, to attribute transformative power to the beatific vision is to implicitly accept that instantaneous transformation will happen to every believer, which is why Walls's conclusion that the only way to preserve true humanity in the redeemed is via synergistic purgatory seems inconsistent to me. God is delighted to change me as I behold him in glory.

This is the hope that Protestantism has long affirmed, and the joyful anticipation that undergirds the traditional evangelical understanding of a believer's experience upon death. This is also consistent with John's description in the passage just discussed. In 1 John 3:1, he exuberantly declares, "Behold what manner of love the Father has bestowed upon us, that we should be called children of God! Therefore, the world does not know us because it did not know Him." At this point, John is explaining that a result of God's saving love is a different status in the world; we are children of God and different from those around us (which entails, I conclude, a moral component since "the world does not know us;" we are different!). After making this sweeping declaration, John then states in 3:2 that what happens to us next is even greater than what happened when we became believers. "Beloved," he writes, "now we are children of God; and it has not yet been revealed what we shall be, but we know that when He is revealed we shall be like Him."

Notice the transition. In this life we are children of God, in the next we will become even more.

Where is the pause for purgatory? If it is there, John certainly omits it, speaking only of transformation that comes when we see God. He transforms us face to face in an instant. If we want to emphasize the necessity of seeking purification in preparation for the beatific vision, then let us follow John's own directive. In verse 3 he makes clear the need for such preparation, and it is in this life as we consider the blessedness awaiting us: "And everyone who has this hope in Him [viz, that when we see Jesus we will be transformed into greater Christlikeness] purifies himself, just as He is pure." Simply stated, John's argument is different than the pro-purgatory argument. John tells us to purify ourselves now in anticipation of what will happen when we behold the beatific vision, following the logic that God works within us now, will bring us to himself in the future, and when he does, he will complete what he started. Where is purgatory in this logic?

Another objection could be that the passage in John is not necessarily speaking of the moment of death, but of the final appearing of Jesus at his second coming. Okay, let's assume that is correct. My argument still holds, since even if the transformation occurs in that instant, it is still an instantaneous transformation precipitated by beholding the beatific vision. As I stated previously, once it is agreed upon that God instantaneously changes us, the question is no longer if, but when. Those who argue for purgatory as preparation for change, especially since change must be gradual and incremental and synergistic, have a dilemma with the beatific vision. They are basically saying that we need to do some change, since instantaneous change is not really genuine or appropriate for human-divine synergy, and so we need purgatory. However, we cannot do all the change, because God still must instantaneously change us—and will—when we see him in glory. At this point it seems to me the purgatory advocate is holding on for the sake of holding on, since the air is out of the no-instantaneous-change-balloon. I fear that their insistence upon purgatory actually obfuscates the transformative power of seeing God face to face, though I am certain none of them ever intended to do so, and that none will resist an instantaneous change upon beholding the beatific vision.

Before leaving this particular issue, I offer another point of consideration related to God's transformative work in believers that is concomitant with the beatific vision. To help, think for a moment about the difference between analogical and univocal knowledge. Analogical knowledge is a way of knowing by analogy, where what we know of God, for example, is analogous to something or someone else. I know that God is loving by way of analogy, because I know what it means to be loving as a father. Yes, God is love, but I know of this about him through analogies like this one and others. What I don't have is univocal knowledge of God. Univocal knowledge is a qualitatively different type of knowledge that entails an exactness between two things. To have univocal knowledge of God I would have to be different than I am now, able to understand at a deeper level that is the same as God's understanding of himself. I will never have this level of knowledge, and neither will you. We are creatures with limitations. However, there is a time coming when I will have a change in knowledge from what I believe is an analogous type to a univocal type regarding certain truths of the Christian faith, and possible awareness of myself.

This is not an idea I came up with on my own. It comes from Paul, who told the Corinthians about a change that occurs when the "perfect has come" (1 Cor 13:10), which is most likely a reference to being in God's presence in heaven. "For now we see in a mirror dimly," Paul wrote, "but then face to face. Now I know in part, but then I shall know just as I am known" (1 Cor 13:12). Notice the final part of Paul's explanation, where he speaks of a change in our knowledge from "part" to "know[ing] just as [we are] known." When we are with Jesus, our knowledge changes. We know more and differently. Even if knowing more and differently does not entail changing from analogical to univocal knowledge, it does entail a change of some kind. What affects the change? Nothing in Paul's language implies moral transformation as the means to this change in knowledge. Rather, what Paul speaks of is an upgrade in our perceptive capacities and knowledge that is a divine gift. Is it less valuable without first undergoing purgation? I don't think so. Actually, I think this is precisely the kind of gift that one should expect from a loving God who welcomes his children into his transformative presence. God's grace is not destroying human nature in this instance. Rather, grace is perfecting the nature of the redeemed as they behold the beatific vision.

## PURGATORY IS BASED ON CONFUSION WITHIN THE CATECHISM OF THE CATHOLIC CHURCH

My final rational reason to reject purgatory is that the traditional Roman Catholic teaching about it is based on confusing inconsistencies within the *Catechism of the Catholic Church*. The problem arises when one compares the statements of the *Catechism* about what Jesus' death accomplished, especially regarding justification, with the *Catechism's* statements about purgatory.

When discussing the atonement of Jesus, the *Catechism* states that "Jesus atoned for our faults and made satisfaction for our sins to the Father."[2] The language is unequivocal: Jesus' death both addressed the faults of the sinner and made satisfaction with the Father. This is why the *Catechism* elsewhere refers to the death of Jesus as accomplishing "the definitive redemption of men," and states that "this sacrifice of Christ is unique; it completes and surpasses all other sacrifices."[3] The words "definitive" and "completes" are strong indications that the work of Jesus is both full and final in its salvific accomplishment.

Concerning Christ's sacrifice, which, biblically speaking, is for the purification and holiness of the sinner, thereby removing a sinner's condemnation before God (cf. John 3:18; 1 John 1:7), the *Catechism* certainly aligns with the text of the New Testament. Compare John 1:29's description of Jesus as the "Lamb of God who takes away the sins of the world," and Hebrews 10:9's declaration

---

2. *Catechism*, 175.

3. *Catechism*, 174.

that, since Jesus yielded himself to the Father's will in becoming the perfect sacrifice for sin, "we have been sanctified through the offering of the body of Jesus Christ once for all." It would be hard to imagine any words more consistent with the traditional evangelical explanations of the cross work of Jesus, especially in its definitive, all-encompassing sense in relationship to making believers holy and acceptable to God.

However, when these words are compared with the following from the *Catechism* regarding the actions of others in doing works of penance on behalf of those in purgatory, I think we see a contradiction. In spite of the *Catechism's* strong language about Jesus atoning for faults and making satisfaction for sins, purgatory is described for those Christians who are "still imperfectly purified," and in need of postmortem "purification, so as to achieve the holiness necessary to enter the joy of heaven."[4] How are they purified? They are purified through works of penance that they do and/or that others do on their behalf.[5] The difference between the *Catechism's* teaching on justification and its teaching on penance is the crux of the problem. As the *Catechism* states, only through the penance of the person or through the penance done for the person, is it possible to "recover his full spiritual health," and "make satisfaction for or expiate his sins."[6] Which is it? Does Jesus provide spiritual health, make satisfaction for or expiate sins, or is it the work of the persons doing penance?

According to the *Catechism's* teaching discussed above, Jesus' death is definitive and complete, but in discussing penance, which is an essential component to the teaching on purgatory, the *Catechism* teaches that it is human works of penance that make satisfaction and expiation for sin. I find this contradictory, or at least highly problematic and confusing. In this instance, the *Catechism* appears to give with one hand what it takes away with the other. What the *Catechism* states about the significance of Jesus' death

4. *Catechism*, 290.

5. *Catechism*, 291. In this context almsgiving and indulgences are also included.

6. *Catechism*, 407.

in dealing with sin and the exemplary nature of his sacrifice seem wholly incongruent with the Roman teaching on purgatory. I suspect this disconnect represents a *bona fide non sequitur*. I am not convinced that these two teachings from the *Catechism* can be reconciled without some type of equivocation, and thus my concern that there really is a contradiction. At the very least there certainly appears to be an internal problem with the *Catechism's* teaching regarding the sacrifice of Jesus and the need for purgatory.

## CONCLUSION

In concluding this chapter, I need to make a confession. I chose to focus on the rational problems I see in the purgatory argument, at least in part, because Walls has made much of what he thinks is the logical consistency of purgatory. His chief work on the topic even includes the word logic in the title—*Purgatory: The Logic of Total Transformation*. Though Walls and other purgatory-evangelicals and their traditional Roman Catholic cobelligerents do argue logically, the problem I attempted to bring out in this chapter is that some of their premises are flawed, and so they introduce logical inconsistencies that undermine the strength of their arguments for purgatory. My cheeky assessment is that perhaps I should rename this chapter "The Blessed Zap: The Logic of Instantaneous Glorification!"

# 6

# So That Settles It, Right?

A Concluding Invitation to
Constructive Dialogue about Purgatory

As I STATED ABOVE, I am a hat-in-hand evangelical. I am not
defensive, but I will defend my convictions that purgatory is a
bad doctrine. I am not argumentative, but I do believe there are
reasonable arguments against purgatory. Some have even accused
me of making my arguments against purgatory in a haranguing
manner, with a lecturing and diatribe-like tone and approach.
Perhaps this is true, but I am a pastor-theologian. The first word in
that description is my heartbeat, and I make no apologies for pur-
suing scholarship for the sake of the pastoral calling. I approach
my scholarship from the perspective of one who has stood in the
pulpit week in and week out for decades and been responsible for
shepherding souls for which I will someday give an account. My
tone is often exhortatory and direct, and I think it should be in
such an important instance. But I am still offering an argument
that I wish to discuss with others for the sake of truth.

Further, as a minister in congregations for over three decades, I have learned how important it is to have clarity about final
life issues, and that Christians often falter precisely at the point

of understanding and explaining what they believe and why they believe it when it comes to personal eschatology. This is more than a simple academic consideration to me, and I am sure it is more than that to pro-purgatory teachers. I do not pretend to have made the best statement on the subject, as I am sure the statement I have made can be improved, has gaps in presentation, and will need to be worked and reworked over the years. However, it is a contribution to the dialogue about personal destinies and the Christian life. It is in that spirit of contribution that I offer the following areas of agreement as well as a suggestion for further dialogue, and that is a suggestion I take seriously.

## AREAS OF AGREEMENT

All parties to this discussion agree on who God is: Father, Son, and Holy Spirit. We also agree that salvation is only by grace and through the cross of Jesus. This is not to reduce the differences between Roman Catholic and Protestant approaches to only matters of authority or justification, but we do agree on the Trinity and the necessity of Christ's atoning death. We also agree that Jesus is going to return one day and that we are to live faithfully in our respective generations as his ambassadors of grace. Specific to personal eschatology, we all agree—historic evangelicals, pro-purgatory evangelicals, and Roman Catholics—that heaven is for saints and that how we live this life will affect our experience in the next. We also agree that there is a judgment coming and that in the final resurrection every believer will behold the glorious beatific vision.

## WHERE DO WE GO FROM HERE?

At the risk of appearing to weaken my own case against purgatory, I must emphasize again that I know that this is not the final word. Several areas of discussion are possible. How does our understanding of time in this life differ from a postmortem reckoning of time, and how might this relate to the transformation that happens at death? Is it possible that a moment of transformation is both instantaneous and purgative? I don't think so, at least not in terms that would support any of the current conceptions of purgatory, but this is a crucial point to consider. Why have many capable moral apologists like Lewis, Owen, Taylor, and Baggett opted for some type of purgatory teaching, and what can traditional evangelicals learn from them? These and other questions offer opportunities for further dialogue, and I invite my pro-purgatory interlocutors to meet me at the table for the discussion. Until then, I will continue to affirm that to be absent from the body is to be present with the Lord, and gloriously so! Soli Deo Gloria!

# Appendix
## When Will I See Jesus?

## AGAINST PURGATORY AND
## FOR THE BEATIFIC VISION

In this appendix, I summarize my arguments against purgatory by bringing together in list form the biblical, theological, and rational reasons presented in the previous chapters. After that, I present five theses that offer a positive statement of what happens when a believer dies. Presenting the material this way is intended to aid in quickly accessing the gist of the arguments against purgatory and to summarize my understanding of the traditional evangelical position.

## AGAINST PURGATORY: A SUMMARY

From a textual perspective, purgatory is not taught in Scripture, nor is it necessary to conclude that purgatory is the most reasonable interpretation of the key apocryphal text referenced in the *Catechism of the Catholic Church* (2 Macc 12:38–46).

From a theological perspective, purgatory directly contradicts the teaching of Paul in 2 Corinthians 5:7–8, it diminishes the importance of the imputation of Jesus' active and passive obedience to the believer, and it does not sufficiently explain the account of Jesus and the thief on the cross in Luke 23:39–43.

From a rational perspective, purgatory creates an unnecessary opposition between human freedom and instantaneous glorification of the believer, it obfuscates the significance of the beatific vision and its transformative effect and contradicts its own insistence on the need to be transformed prior to seeing God face to face, and it proceeds from logical inconsistencies in the *Catechism of the Catholic Church*.

## FOR THE BEATIFIC VISION: FIVE THESES

1. When God instantaneously changes a person's nature at the moment of salvation, he transfers them from the kingdom of darkness to the kingdom of God and begins a process that entails declarative justification, progressive sanctification, and final glorification.

2. In this life, the believer is to cooperate with the grace of God in working out the implications of the salvation received at his conversion, including learning to yield himself to the transformative work of the Holy Spirit.

3. At the moment of death, a believer is absent from the body and present with Jesus, immediately enfolded into the communion of saints in heavenly glory and receiving the first fruits of the eternal reward of the faithful.

4. When the believer sees God in glory, he is immediately changed, becoming like Jesus in a mysterious moment of transformation and enjoying the blessedness of heavenly rest and respite while awaiting the final resurrection.

5. When the final resurrection occurs, the believer receives a glorified body and will forever be with the Lord in the new heavens and earth among the saints of all ages, where each one is perfectly glorified by the gracious initiative of God.

# Bibliography

Allison, Gregg. "What's the Difference?" *Credo* 3:1 (January 2013) 18–25.

Baker, Todd L. *Exodus from Rome Volume 1: A Biblical and Historical Critique of Roman Catholicism.* Bloomington: iUniverse, 2014.

Bathrellos, Demetrios. "Love, Purification, and Forgiveness versus Justice, Punishment, and Satisfaction: The Debates on Purgatory and the Forgiveness of Sins at the Council of Ferrara–Florence." *Journal of Theological Studies* 65:1 (April 2014) 78–121.

Bernard, Justin D. "Purgatory and the Dilemma of Sanctification." *Faith and Philosophy* 4 (2007) 311–30.

Bloesch, Donald G. *The Last Things: Resurrection, Judgment, Glory.* Downers Grove: InterVarsity, 2004.

Blomberg, Craig L. *Matthew.* New American Commentary 22. Nashville: Broadman and Holman, 1992. Kindle ed.

Calvin, John. *The Institutes of the Christian Religion.* Translated by Henry Beveridge. First published 1845. http://www.ccel.org/ccel/calvin/institutes.html.

———. *Soul Sleep.* CreateSpace, 2011. Kindle ed.

Casey, John. *After Lives: A Guide to Heaven, Hell, and Purgatory.* New York: Oxford University Press, 2009.

Castaldo, Chris. "Purgatory's Logic, History, and Meaning." *Credo* 3:1 (January 2013) 34–42.

*Catechism of the Catholic Church.* 2nd ed. New York: Doubleday, 1992.

Cevetello, J. F. X. "Purgatory: In the Bible." In *New Catholic Encyclopedia,* edited by Thomas Carson. 2nd ed. Detroit: Thompson Gale, 2003.

Christian, Ed. "The Rich Man and Lazarus, Abraham's Bosom, and the Biblical Penalty *Karet* ('Cut Off')." *Journal of the Evangelical Theological Society* 61:3 (2018) 513–24.

Ciampa, Roy E., and Brian S. Rosner. *The First Letter to the Corinthians.* Pillar New Testament Commentary. Grand Rapids: Eerdmans, 2010.

Crockett, William V., editor. *Four Views on Hell.* Grand Rapids: Zondervan. 1992.

D'Costa, Gavin. "The Descent into Hell as a Solution for the Problem of the Fate of Unevangelized Non-Christians: Balthasar's Hell, the Limbo of the Fathers, and Purgatory." *International Journal of Systematic Theology* 11:2 (April 2009) 146–71.

De Chirico, Leonardo. *Evangelical Theological Perspectives on Post-Vatican II Roman Catholicism.* Bern: Peter Lang, 2003.

de Sales, Francis. *The Catholic Controversy.* Translated by Henry B. Mackey. Rockford: TAN Books, 1989.

Egan, Harvey D. "In Purgatory We Shall All Be Mystics." *Theological Studies* 73:4 (December 2012) 870–89.

Enns, Paul. *The Moody Handbook of Theology.* Rev. and exp. ed. Chicago: Moody, 2014. Kindle ed.

Evener, Vincent. "Wittenberg's Wandering Spirits: Discipline and the Dead in the Reformation." *Church History* 84:3 (September 2015) 531.

Fee, Gordon D. *The First Epistle to the Corinthians.* Rev. ed. New International Commentary on the New Testament. Grand Rapids: Eerdmans, 2014.

Fenn, Richard K. *The Persistence of Purgatory.* Cambridge: Cambridge University Press, 1995.

Garland, David E. *2 Corinthians.* New American Commentary 29. Nashville: Holman, 2014. Kindle ed.

Geisler, Norman L. *Systematic Theology.* Minneapolis: Bethany House, 2011.

Geisler, Norman L., and Ralph E. MacKenzie. *Roman Catholics and Evangelicals: Agreements and Differences.* Grand Rapids: Baker, 1995.

Gregory the Great. *Dialogues.* Translated by T. W. Re-edited by Edmund G. Gardner. London: Philip Lee Warner, 1811. Online at http://www.tertullian.org/fathers/index.htm#Gregory_Dialogues.

Grudem, Wayne. *Systematic Theology: An Introduction to Biblical Doctrine.* Grand Rapids: Zondervan, 1994.

Hahn, Scott. "Purgatory, Holy Fire." Program 14, in module 4 of *Catholic Adult Education,* by Scott Hahn and Kimberly Hahn. Transcript of DVD video recording. Manassas, VA: Catholic Resource Network, 1994. Online at http://zuserver2.star.ucl.ac.uk/~vgg/rc/aplgtc/hahn/m4/pg.html.

Hahn, Scott, and Kimberly Hahn. *Rome Sweet Home: Our Journey to Catholicism.* San Francisco: Ignatius, 2009. Kindle ed.

Hanna, Edward. "Purgatory." New Advent. In *Catholic Encyclopedia,* vol. 12. New York: Robert Appleton, 1911. Online at http://www.newadvent.org/cathen/12575a.htm.

Haydock, George L. *Commentary on the New Testament of Our Lord and Savior Jesus Christ.* First published 1859. Veritatis Splendor, 2012. Kindle ed.

Hill, Jonathan. *The History of Christian Thought.* Downers Grove, IL: InterVarsity, 2003.

Hodge, Charles. *Commentary on 2 Corinthians.* First published 1859. Titus Books, 2013. Kindle ed.

Judisch, Neal. "Sanctification, Satisfaction, and the Purpose of Purgatory." *Faith and Philosophy* 26 (209) 167–85.

Keil, C. F., and Franz Delitzsch. *Commentary on the Minor Prophets*. Translated by James Martin. First published 1864. Amazon, 2014. Kindle.

Lance, H. Darrell. "What Is Theological Research?" *Theological Education* 16:2 (1980) 465–71.

Le Goffe, Jacques. *The Birth of Purgatory*. Translated by Arthur Goldhammer. Chicago: University of Chicago Press, 1984.

Lewis, C. S. *The Complete C. S. Lewis Signature Classics*. San Francisco: HarperSanFrancisco, 2002.

Leyshon, Gareth. "The Purpose of Purgatory: Expiation or Maturation?" BTh diss., St John's Seminary, 2005. http://www.drgareth.info/Purgatory.pdf.

Luther, Martin. *Lectures on Genesis Chapters 21–25*. Vol. 4 of *Luther's Works*, edited by Jaroslav Pelikan. St. Louis: Concordia, 1964.

———. "Of Purgatory." In *The Table-Talk of Martin Luther*, translated by William Hazlitt. Philadelphia: Lutheran Publication Society, n.d.. http://www.ccel.org/ccel/luther/tabletalk.v.xix.html.

Machen, Chase E. "The Concept of Purgatory in England." PhD diss., University of North Texas, 2010. UMI 3436537.

McGrath, Alister E. *Historical Theology: An Introduction to the History of Christian Thought*. Malden, MA: Blackwell 1998.

Mitchell, Dan. *The Book of First Corinthians: Christianity in a Hostile Culture*. Twenty-First Century Biblical Commentary Series. Chattanooga, TN: AMG, 2009.

Montague, George T. *First Corinthians*. Catholic Commentary on Sacred Scripture. Grand Rapids: Baker Academic, 2011. Kindle ed.

More, Thomas. *The Supplication of Souls*. Originally published 1529. Translated by Mary Gottschalk. New York: Scepter, 2002.

Moreira, Isabel. *Heaven's Purge: Purgatory in Late Antiquity*. Oxford: Oxford University Press, 2010.

Oden, Thomas C. *Classic Christianity: A Systematic Theology*. New York: HarperCollins, 1992.

Olsen, Roger E. *The Mosaic of Christian Belief: Twenty Centuries of Unity & Diversity*. Downers Grove, IL: InterVarsity, 2002.

Ratzinger, Joseph. *Eschatology: Death and Eternal Life*. Translated by Michael Waldstein. 2nd ed. Washington, DC: Catholic University of America Press, 1988.

Robinson, Jeff. "Martin Luther on the Doctrine of Purgatory." *Credo* 3:1 (January 2013) 43.

Salkeld, Brett David. "A Creation Refined by Love: The Value of Purgatory for Ecumenical Dialogue." MA thesis, University of St. Michael's College, 2008. ProQuest MR4316.

———. *Can Catholics and Evangelicals Agree about Purgatory and the Last Judgment?* New York: Paulist, 2011.

Schaff, Philip. *History of the Christian Church: The Complete Eight Volumes in One*. Harrington, DE: Delmarva, 2012. Kindle ed.

Skotnicki, Andrew. "God's Prisoners: Penal Confinement and the Creation of Purgatory." *Modern Theology* 22:1 (January 2006) 85–110.

Staples, Tim. "Is Purgatory in the Bible?" Catholic Answers, January 17, 2014. https://www.catholic.com/magazine/online-edition/is-purgatory-in-the-bible.

Stein, Robert A. *Luke.* New American Commentary 24. Nashville: Broadman and Holman, 1993.

Stegman, Thomas D. *Second Corinthians.* Catholic Commentary on Sacred Scripture. Grand Rapids: Baker Academic, 2011. Kindle ed.

Stewart, Don. "Is There Any Biblical Support for Purgatory?" https://www.blueletterbible.org/faq/don_stewart/don_stewart_123.cfm.

Smith, Ralph Alan. *The Eternal Covenant: How the Trinity Reshapes Covenant Theology.* Moscow, ID: Canon, 2003.

Taylor, Mark. *1 Corinthians.* New American Commentary 28. Nashville: Broadman and Holman, 2014. Kindle ed.

Tertullian. *A Treatise on the Soul.* In *Ante-Nicene Fathers,* vol. 3, edited by Philip Schaff and Alan Menzies. Grand Rapids: Eardmans, n.d. Online at http://www.ccel.org/ccel/schaff/anf03.iv.xi.lviii.html.

Thiel, John E. *Icons of Hope: The "Last Things" in Catholic Imagination.* Notre Dame, IN: University of Notre Dame Press, 2013.

———. "Time, Judgment, and Competitive Spirituality: A Reading in the Development of the Doctrine of Purgatory." *Theological Studies* 69:4 (December 2008) 741–85.

Townsend, John T. "1 Corinthians 3:15 and the School of Shammai." *Harvard Theological Review* 61:3 (July 1968) 500–504.

Vander Laan, David. "The Sanctification Argument for Purgatory." *Faith and Philosophy* 24 (2007) 331–39.

Vyhmeister, Nancy J., and Terry D. Robertson. *Quality Research Papers: For Students of Religion and Theology.* 3rd ed. Grand Rapids: Zondervan, 2014.

Walls, Jerry L. *Heaven, Hell, and Purgatory: Rethinking the Things that Matter Most.* Grand Rapids: Brazos, 2015.

———. *Hell: The Logic of Damnation.* Notre Dame, IN: University of Notre Dame Press, 1992.

———. *Purgatory: The Logic of Total Transformation.* Oxford: Oxford University Press, 2012.

Wesley, John. *2 Corinthians: Explanatory Notes and Commentary.* Hargreaves, 2014. Kindle ed.

*Westminster Confession of Faith.* 1646. Online at https://reformed.org/documents/index.html?mainframe=https://reformed.org/documents/westminster_conf_of_faith.html.

Wilkins, Michael J. *Matthew.* NIV Application Commentary. Grand Rapids: Zondervan, 2004.

Wilkins, Steve, and Duane Garner, editors. *The Federal Vision.* Monroe, LA: Athanasius, 2004.

Wright, N. T. *The Resurrection of the Son of God*. Christian Origins and the Question of God 3. Minneapolis: Fortress, 2003.

———. "Rethinking the Tradition." In *For All the Saints?: Remembering the Christian Departed*, 20–46. London: SPCK, 2003. Online at http://ntwrightpage.com/Wright_Rethinking_Tradition.htm.

# Subject Index

# Scripture Index

www.ingramcontent.com/pod-product-compliance
Lightning Source LLC
Chambersburg PA
CBHW060422090426
42734CB00011B/2405